Also by Martin Mull and Allen Rucker:
THE HISTORY OF WHITE PEOPLE IN AMERICA

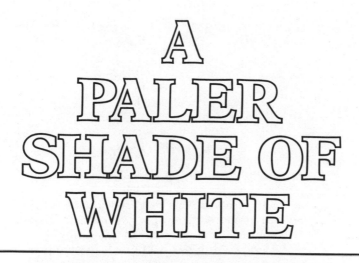

A PALER SHADE OF WHITE

THE HISTORY OF WHITE PEOPLE
IN AMERICA, VOLUME II

MARTIN MULL
AND
ALLEN RUCKER

A Perigee Book

Perigee Books
are published by
The Putnam Publishing Group
200 Madison Avenue
New York, NY 10016

Typeset by Fisher Composition, Inc.
Photographs courtesy of FPG International.

Library of Congress Cataloging-in-Publication Data

Mull, Martin
The history of white people in America.

"A Perigee book."
Bibliography: v. [1] p.
Contents: [1] [without special title] — v. 2. A paler
shade of white.
1. United States—Social life and customs—1971–
Anecdotes, facetiae, satire, etc.   I. Rucker, Allen.
II. Title.
E169.02.M85   1985   973.9   85-12464
ISBN 0-399-51193-8 (pbk. : v.1)
ISBN 0-399-51300-0 (pbk. : v.2)

Printed in the United States of America
1   2   3   4   5   6   7   8   9   10

Acknowledgments

Many people contributed to this work, in substance and in spirit. They include: Harry Shearer, Fred Willard, Mary Kay Place, Kevin Bright, Wendy Haas-Mull, Ann-Marie Rucker, Charles Engel, Janet Saunders, Nancy Cushing-Jones, John Hornick, Peter Giagni, and Ted Steinberg. Thank you all.

To Blaine and Maggie Rose.
From your alleged fathers.

Contents

Introduction

Frankly, we thought we covered it pretty well in Book One. Boy, are our white faces red! In the scant twelve months since the initial publication of *The History of White People in America*, a mandate has risen from the American reading public. Every day, as we walk along the well-manicured, elm-lined streets of White America, we are accosted, in the nicest possible way, by pleas for greater understanding.

"Isn't there more to the story of White People?" "How about a second book with more pictures?" "Prove it!" "How do you get into something like writing a book?" "Did my uncle's lawyer call you? There's one guy in your book just like him, and he wants to settle out of court."

Clearly we struck a nerve. We barely cracked open the front door of White Consciousness, and a whole crowd came busting in, looking for the refreshments. What began as a simple weekend search for personal identity has now become an enduring obligation to stand up and speak out. There are white people out there, a lot of them, and their stories must be told.

Some say we are wasting our time, that White Culture as we know it is dying out, and not a minute too soon. Maybe so. Maybe this is all just an elaborate death rattle for a bunch of pathetic squareheads who couldn't keep up and didn't have enough sense to come in out of the rain. Maybe we're barking up the wrong tree here and should be turning our attention to *Market Opportunities in the Pacific Rim* or *Sex with Your In-Laws*, useful subjects with a built-in readership.

We disagree, and we have gathered the following tales of whiteness as our defense. The subject is far from exhausted. Book One was just the tip of the iceberg, and there is tons of ice left. White People love ice. They put it in wine, even red wine. They fill coolers with it, skate on it, and chip it away with screwdrivers when it builds up in their freezers or on the windshields of their Oldsmobiles on bone-chilling mornings. Ask any reputable white hostess the cardinal rule of party-giving and she will tell you without hesitation, "Never run out of ice."

We don't plan to.

MM and AR
July, 1986

1

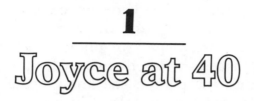

Joyce at 40

If Joyce Harrison was any whiter, she wouldn't have a navel. She dusts her light bulbs, irons her place mats, and her weekly menu planning has single-handedly caused the Kraft Corporation stock to split several times. She keeps the dishwasher on "energy-saver," writes thank-you notes before she's even unwrapped the gift, and makes sure that every room in the house has a night-light. As her husband Hal puts it, "If she lost twenty or thirty pounds, she'd be perfect."

On this particular Sunday Joyce Harrison is celebrating her fortieth birthday.

No one in Edgewood Terrace (the development where the Harrisons make their home) has a rooster, so the first sounds that greeted Joyce on "birthday morning" were those of her husband rumbling in the shower.

"You okay?" she said, instinctively concerned.

"I'm fine, I just wouldn't come in here right now."

Joyce sat up in bed and began taking out her rollers.

"By the way, happy birthday," he added.

Having made the bed, Joyce entered the bathroom tentatively and, after opening the window just a crack, began to "put on her face." She based, blushed, brushed, tweezed, and sprayed herself into the person she knew herself to be. Then, after cleaning Hal's whiskers out of the sink with a Kleenex and a little Comet, she went to the kitchen to make her birthday breakfast.

Joyce filled the Mr. Coffee machine and thought for a moment about the Joe DiMaggio commercial that had convinced Hal they needed one. Her brain then took the obvious synapse from Joe DiMaggio to his late wife. "How old would Marilyn be today if she hadn't . . ." she wondered aloud. "Fifty? Fifty-two?" She stared blankly into the open refrigerator and suddenly caught a glimpse of herself in the stretched Saran Wrap covering the remnants of last night's broccoli. Not bad for forty, she said to herself as she wiped the lipstick off her teeth.

In a jiffy the Formica kitchen table was filled with a smorgasbord of white breakfast goodies. Joyce knew the importance of a good breakfast. As Joyce's two-hundred-and-eighty-pound sister used to say, "It's the most important meal of the morning."

On this special Sunday, Joyce brought out the works. Pop Tarts, Frosted Flakes, Kix, cholesterol-free Egg Beaters, frozen waffles, raisin bread, Brown 'N Serve sausages, margarine,

14

nondairy creamer, and an enormous bowl of white sugar.

She poured herself some coffee, adjusted her apron so Mr. Happy Face was dead-center over her heart, and sat down at the table awaiting her starving brood. It's an awful lot of food, she thought. Maybe I should put in the leaf.

Her deliberation as to whether to use the "special occasions" table leaf ended the moment her husband bounded into the kitchen wearing only his checkered golf slacks. "Honey, where in the hell is my golf shirt?" he boomed.

"Which one, sweetheart? You've got hundreds of them," said Joyce as she placed the margarine stick into her favorite little ceramic cow dish.

"You know which one," he boomed again. "My *golf* shirt, for Christ's sake. My *lucky* golf shirt!"

Joyce began nervously cutting the margarine stick into individual pats. "You're not talking about that old yellow one that was all ripped out under the arms, are you?"

Hal closed his eyes in pain. "What do you mean *was*, Joyce?"

Joyce took four slices of raisin bread and arranged them on a platter, placing a little margarine pat dead-center on each slice.

"I was going to surprise you and get you a new one tomorrow, Hal. The May Company is having a sale. Besides, I didn't think you would be playing golf today." Hal sat with his jaw clenched and looked out the kitchen window at what was rapidly becoming one of the finest golf days imaginable.

"Well, I'm sure as hell not going to play *good* golf today. That's for damned sure. Not without my lucky shirt." He rose from his chair like a man losing a lottery spin, and headed back to the bedroom.

"I'm sorry, darling. It just looked so ratty," she called after him.

Hal turned on his heels, a fresh thought in his mind. "And what made you think that I wasn't going to play golf today, anyway? Huh? I played golf when *I* turned forty. What's the big difference? Besides, you were the one that said you'd just as soon forget all about this birthday!"

Joyce slumped into her chair. "I don't know," she said, "I just thought for a minute that today we might . . . I don't know."

Hal sat himself down opposite her, pulled his chair up to where his face was no more than three inches from hers. "Okay, Joyce, here goes."

He then inched even closer and began to sing at the top of his lungs. As he sang he became angrier and angrier, until by song's end his face was redder than a fat man on a hike.

"Happy birthday to you
Happy birthday to you
Happy birthday Mrs. Doesn't-ask-
Permission-before-she-throws-
Someone's-favorite-golf-shirt-out!
Happy birthday to you."

Hal then began clapping maniacally. The sound of the applause was augmented by the four little hands of their two children, who had been watching all of this from the doorway.

"Mom, is it really your birthday?" said little Debbie, age sixteen.

"Yes, it is," said Mom.

"Honest to God?" said little Tommy, age fourteen.

"Honest to God," said Mom.

Debbie rushed to her father's side. "Daddy, you've got to drive Tommy and me to Thrifty's right away!"

Hal headed back down the hallway to the bedroom. "You work it out with them, Joyce. I'll drive 'em, but you work it out."

Joyce turned to her children, announced that "no one is going anywhere until you've at least had a Pop-Tart," and followed her husband into the bedroom.

Tommy put a Brown 'N Serve sausage in the toaster to see if it would work, and Debbie licked the icing off a piece of raisin bread and threw the rest down the disposal.

It was still only eight-thirty.

By ten o'clock life was pretty well back to normal. Joyce located Hal's favorite golf shirt in the Goodwill bag and, with the help of some iron-on Magic Mender tape, was able to insure that the armpits would hold out for another eighteen holes. Hal, instantly more amiable once his prized shirt was rejuvenated, managed a little

forehead kiss for the "birthday girl" and agreed
to drop the kids at Thrifty's if they found their
own way back.

Each child was given five dollars with the im-
plicit understanding that it was to be used only
for a gift for their mother, and the spelled-out
understanding that they would tie up the news-
papers in the basement and clean the dog doo in
the backyard as payback.

As the car pulled out of the driveway, Joyce
could hear the phone ringing.

Joyce knew instantly from the static that it was
her mother and stepfather in Arizona and that
they were in the backyard with the Extend-A-
Phone. Before she could even say hello to them
they began to sing "Happy birthday."

It was a fairly rousing rendition at first with an
attempt at harmony, but when Dad got a cough-
ing fit midway, Mom had to finish up as best she
could. Joyce was very glad to hear from her. They
were as close as any two white people could be.
Here's what was said:

JOYCE: Thanks, Mom, and thank you, Arnold.

MOM: He can't hear you, honey. He's in the
bathroom getting his Romilar.

JOYCE: Is he all right?

MOM: Oh, I don't know, and to tell you the
truth, sometimes I don't even care. The
important thing is how are *you!* This is
your big day!

JOYCE: Well, I'm just fine, Mom. I got your card
yesterday; that was very sweet.

MOM: Oh, I'm so glad it got there in time. You

know, I looked high and low for one with the fuzzy ducks like you like, but the only one that they had was three dollars! Can you imagine that? Three dollars for a birthday card? In fact I showed it to the girl at the shop and asked her if this was a mistake, and she just looked at me. I think she was Spanish. I tell you, Arizona is just crawling with them. You wouldn't recognize the place.

JOYCE: Now, Mom, you . . . remember what you always taught us. "If you can't say something nice about someone . . ."

MOM: I know—"Don't say anything at all." But you *did* like the card?

JOYCE: The turtles were very cute.

MOM: Well, I remembered that you liked turtles, too. I was going to send you a little present, but Jiminy Christmas everything is so expensive today. Did I tell you that I saw a birthday card for three dollars?

JOYCE: Yes, I think you did. Mom, this call has got to be costing you a fortune.

MOM: Well, it's not every day that my little girl turns the big four-O! You know, that's when I had my hysterectomy. How are *you* feeling these days?

JOYCE: Couldn't be better, Mom.

MOM: And Hal and the kids? Debbie and . . .

JOYCE: Tommy, Mom. They're all fine. Everyone's just fine.

MOM: Well, that's *so* good to hear. Now make

sure you don't eat the whole cake your-self!

JOYCE: Oh, Mom.

MOM: I'm only teasing, sweetheart. But *do* make sure you have the addresses of all the people that give you gifts so you can write them thank-you notes.

JOYCE: I always do, Mom.

MOM: Well, it gets important when you get to be our age. Listen, this is costing me a fortune. I'll call again on Easter. I love you.

JOYCE: Me too, Mom. Bye.

Joyce hung up the phone and got her special stationery and wrote a thank-you note to her mom for the call. She had already written one for the card.

Hal pulled the Country Squire into the Thrifty's parking lot. "Okay, kids, get something for your mother, and then straight home. It's her birthday and someone should be there."

"We know, Daddy," chirped Debbie.

Hal sped away and the two children made a beeline for the store. Debbie went straight to the pay phone to call her friends and Tommy went straight to the magazines. Specifically, the "men's" magazines.

Before she knew it, Debbie had fed all but fifty cents of her five dollars into the phone. Thinking fast, she made the following deal with her brother. She wouldn't tell that he was reading

Playboy in the store if he would give her his five dollars and she'd get something from both of them. Tommy agreed and Debbie proceeded to purchase the world's smallest bottle of Vitabath bath oil. It was five dollars and forty-eight cents. After she purchased the Vitabath and received her two pennies' change, she cleverly removed the price sticker from the ten-dollar bottle of Vitabath bath oil and stuck it on her package.

The two children began to hitchhike home.

Hal Harrison was already late for his golf match but, even though he was only a mile and a half from the club, he decided that he just "couldn't take it anymore." Apparently the usual pregame anxiety and unseasonably warm weather had conspired in the form of underarm wetness, which melted the glue of the Magic Mender tape. Now, with every turn of the wheel he could feel the tugging, sticking, and hair pulling in his pits. He decided to go home and change.

Joyce Harrison finished her thank-you note to her mom, a three-pager, and noticed a strange smell in the kitchen. She tried several different air fresheners, but nothing seemed to do the trick. It was the smell of burning pork.

Hal gunned the Country Squire down the highway, pausing only for a brief minute or so at Thrifty's to pick up something for his wife. He bought her a five-dollar-and-forty-eight-cent bottle of Vitabath oil.

The children got a ride from a Mister Donut

truck that dropped them four blocks from Edge-wood Terrace.

Joyce finally located the problem. It was the Brown 'N Serve sausage that Tommy had earlier placed in the toaster. She decided to get it out, pronto. She grabbed a fork and plunged it into the toaster hoping to stab the little piggy on her first attempt. She must have hit a wire in there or something, because what happened next made her hair go straight, her skin turn a lovely light blue, and her eyes turn into burnt Cheerios. She froze for a moment, then did something she had never done before, and hasn't since. She ran into the bathroom, took off all of her clothes, and started taking nude Polaroid pictures of herself.

Debbie and Tommy were not that big on exercise, so they elected to try to hitch the last four blocks as well. As Hal Harrison approached Edgewood Terrace, he saw his little ones with their thumbs out and screeched to a halt beside them.

"We knew it was you, Daddy," lied Debbie.

"Like hell you did," said Hal, and the children piled into the car.

As the family approached the driveway to their home, they got their first hint that something was wrong. All of Hal's golf shirts were strewn across the lawn.

They ran into the house, each with their respective bottle of Vitabath bath oil.

Hal was screaming. "Joyce, what in the hell is going on here?" There was no response.

When they finally discovered her she was lying flat on her back in the middle of the rec room staring at nude Polaroids of herself that she had neatly tacked dead-center in the middle of the tiles of their acoustic ceiling. She had a large, bright red "40" written in lipstick on her stomach and was smiling radiantly.

———

Three years later, after several dozen more shocks that utilized equipment much more sophisticated than a toaster, the people at Restful Hills decided it was time for Joyce to come home, where she remains to this day, ironing her Handi Wipes and vacuuming the dog dish.

2

Death in Venice II

A day at Cedar Point Amusement Park, a half day at Euclid Beach Amusement Park, and two weeks at Black Bottom National Park just outside of Pittsburgh—that pretty much sums up twenty-five years of vacationing for the Fergusons.

But now, with the kids grown and gone, and the Postal Service pension to lean on, Carl and Dorothy decided to take a very big step for white people. They decided to see Europe.

Carl would do all of the planning, both economic and itineral. Dorothy did all of the packing and "travel-tip" gathering. She kept all of her tips in a special little book. It was roughly six by eight inches, covered in padded blue vinyl, and over two hundred pages long by departure time. The cover of her little book had a lovely silk-screened image of the Eiffel Tower emblazoned on it with little embedded rhinestones to indicate the lights. She got it from a catalogue along with a hundred little iron-on name tags for their clothes and a hummingbird feeder.

Space obviously does not permit reprinting her entire journal of tips. However, space does permit boiling it down to what she called the "Ten Commandments."

1. *Do* keep a watchful eye on your passport at all times. Some of these people would give their right arm to come to America under a phony name.
2. *Don't* go to the Moulin Rouge. It's a waste of money. It's a very dirty show and you won't understand a word of it.
3. *Do* buy those ready-made, prepackaged photographic slides of the city. They are usually right next to the postcards. There's always a good chance that your own pictures won't come out.
4. *Don't* order anything to eat that you haven't had before.
5. *Do* take something from the hotel, an ashtray, a towel, what have you. They expect it and write it off.
6. *Don't* go anywhere that doesn't have a sign in the window that says, "We speak English." You could end up trying to eat a fish with its eyes wide open.
7. *Do* try to speak their language. It is a courtesy that they really enjoy.
8. *Don't* miss the Roman ruins. They're already shot and may not be there forever.
9. *Do* give your name, address, and home phone

    number to anyone you meet so that they can become your houseguest if they ever come to the U.S.A.

10. *Don't* ever let them forget that if it wasn't for the bravery of our GIs in 1944, they wouldn't even be here.

Needless to say there were hundreds of other entries in Dorothy's book. Things like, "Here's where to buy those adorable little coasters with the cats on them," and "Always ask for rare in England," but the previous ten were their Bible.

Carl did his homework, too. He talked to every travel agent in town, actually striking up a friendship with two of them. The first was a retired bandleader who would constantly say that he never really minded the Milwaukee winters; the other guy was an Egyptian man who had bleached his hair blond, hoping to blend in.

Carl made the final deal with the Egyptian fellow. The whole tour came to four hundred dollars.

Here was the deal: the Fergusons had to leave anytime between midnight and four AM on a Thursday, stay at least a day and a half, and be willing to fly standby on an Air Force jet for return passage. They would leave Akron, Ohio, and stop briefly in Cleveland, Buffalo, Erie, Scranton, Kennedy, Portland, and then London.

The entire trip took just over eighteen hours, counting layovers. The Fergusons were fairly bushed by the time they reached London's Heathrow Airport and slightly annoyed at having to wait three and a half hours in the customs line. The problem was not with the Fergusons. The problem was with the group just ahead of them in the line: a Laotian soccer team, nineteen members strong, and none of them with any identification whatsoever. Finally it was agreed by all parties that the team should be rerouted to Ireland, where they could catch a flight back to Laos. Begrudgingly, they all picked up their string bags filled with potatoes, yak butter, and soccer balls, and headed for Aer Lingus. It was now time for the Fergusons to enter Europe officially.

It was with renewed vigor that Carl and Dorothy crossed the "please wait here" line and approached the customs official. Carl was the first to break the international ice. "Top o' the mornin' to you, Guv-nor," he chirped in his idea of an English accent. "Pip pip," he added. Not getting the warm handshake or possible hug that he expected, Carl quickly demurred. "I'm only kidding with the accent," he said. "I'm an American. It's our first time here, but I have to tell you I agreed with Churchill during the war."

Dorothy did her best to soften the moment by adding, "And we think that Princess Di is just as cute as a bug!"

The customs official quickly scanned their pristine passports and uttered his first words. "Is this for gainful employment or is it a holiday?"

"Well, let's see, it's June the ninth. I don't think that's a holiday. Unless somebody famous in your country died then," said Dorothy.

"It must be a holiday," Carl chimed in. "I haven't been gainfully employed since 1972. I'm on a Postal Service pension. It's enough to get by. Our country takes care of its people, but I'll just bet you that yours does, too. You all look and act so much like us in a lot of ways."

The customs official never said another word; he simply stamped their passports with great force and directed them toward the baggage claim with a yellowed finger.

The Fergusons only spent two nights at Holmsbly House. Carl couldn't figure out the shower, none of their appliances fit in the socket, and Dorothy became progressively more nauseated every time they "went down the wrong side of the road." They decided to get on with it and go to Paris.

The last thing that Carl did before departure for France was to give the English skycap eighty dollars' worth of English money. "Here, maybe this makes sense to you. I can't figure it, and I don't need it," he proclaimed.

The last thing Dorothy did was buy some ready-made slides of the changing of the guard. They were right there next to the postcards.

Carl slept most of the way to Paris. Dorothy wrote her first postcard. It was to her friend in Ocala, Florida, a widow who had found a new life in coat-hanger art. "All you need is coat hangers, pliers, and a little imagination," she would tell the admirers of her little wiry reindeer.

Here is what Dorothy wrote to her friend:

Dear Gwennie,

Well, we didn't get to see the Queen! I didn't really think we would. As for the food I can't really say. Carl and I ate in the room the whole time so Carl could put it all on the Visa and not have to figure out tips. I think their money is metric or something. Well, it's off to gay Paree, and don't worry I've still got those pictures of your little coat-hanger reindeers, and if I run into some rich European artistic type I'm going to show them to him, believe you me! Hope you haven't had one of those headaches in a while.

Bonjours,

Dorothy and Carl

Paris was a different story. They stayed at a Holiday Inn and enjoyed all of the amenities, including an English-speaking staff and organized tours of the sights. At six AM they, along with eight other retired Americans, would pile into a Dodge step-van and take off for some good picture taking. Window seats were drawn by lottery, and Carl's luck was uncanny. Time after time Carl drew the coveted position right behind the driver. By constantly referring to Paris' most famous landmark as the "Awful Tower," Carl quickly won the hearts of his fellow travelers and dispelled any suspicions of cheating.

On their fourth and final day in Paris, the Fergusons daringly elected to leave the group and do a little looking around on their own. Dorothy was determined to find the place that made those adorable little coasters with the cats on them, and Carl was anxious to try out his French. He had his book of phrases and had been practicing on Dorothy all week. "Look at this," he would boom from the bathroom of their Holiday Inn room, "p-a-r-c is their word for 'park.' So I guess at least they know a damned park when they see one. I'll betcha it's pronounced different, though—they're always pulling that. It's probably 'parse' or 'par-cee' or something."

"You'll have to run that all by me again, honey," his wife shouted back. "I can't hear you over my hair spray."

The entire morning was spent looking for the coasters, but to no avail. Dorothy, not wanting to come back completely empty-handed, did, however, buy some little blown-glass unicorns. She would have continued her search for the elusive coasters after lunch, but the Fergusons had a little setback.

Shortly before noon they felt that familiar rumbling in the tummy and knew that a little lunch was called for. They chose a quaint sidewalk café called Rene's International Sub Shop. Despite the hint that this place probably had waiters who spoke English, the Fergusons decided to "go native," and ordered French toast. Carl looked up the French word for "French toast" and found nothing listed in his phrase book. He then broke it down into "bread," "toast," "eggs," and "hot." Soon the order was placed, and the Fergusons waited and sipped their coffee, constantly adding water to it. When the order arrived it was not exactly what they had in mind. It was squid, covered in raw egg, on a piping hot plate. Starving by now, and not wanting to make waves, the Fergusons did their best to choke down about half of it. They asked for the rest "to go," and about twenty feet outside of the restaurant, in an attempt to be tidy, Dorothy mistakenly placed the doggy bag in a mailbox. It was within minutes that Carl's stomach started its gymnastics. Carl had experienced this before at home. There was the time Dorothy made her own chili, and again the night their block association had its "luau party." It was nothing that a few Rolaids couldn't patch up in a jiffy.

Like a sailor on a turgid sea, Carl set his eye on a fixed point and headed for it. It was a drugstore. Carl quickly scanned his phrase book and, once satisfied that he knew what to say, proceeded to give the French druggist the Gallic translation for, "My stomach has a headache, so I would like to see your testicles, darling." The druggist responded by grabbing a long loaf of very stale bread and clubbing Carl right in the Adam's apple. Horrified, Dorothy dragged her gasping husband from the store. On the way out she noticed the little coasters on the druggist's shelf, but there was no time for that now. The rest of the afternoon would be spent trying to find a whiplash collar in Paris.

Carl's irregular breathing had pretty well subsided by morning, so the decision was made to take their scheduled flight to Italy. Carl, though somewhat contorted by his bulky collar, spent most of the two-hour flight boning up on his Italian phrase book. Dorothy used the opportunity, once again, to write a postcard to her friend Gwennie.

Dear Gwennie,

Well, it's up, up, and away again. This time to Venice, Italy. The bad news is that Carl isn't breathing that well, the good news is that this trip may pay for itself if we filled out the right forms with the American Embassy. It's a long story, too long for a postcard. See you soon.

Carl and Dorothy

P.S. Have you ever thought about doing coathanger unicorns?

Safely ensconced in the famed Garibaldi Hotel in Venice, Carl's rage hit a fever pitch. Apparently his four-hundred-dollar fee was to include a rent-a-car in Italy, and here he was in a city with no roads, not to mention cars. "We're really up shit's canal here!" he would exclaim to his wife.

Carl tossed and turned fitfully all night, so when Dorothy arose the next morning about eight, she decided to let him sleep and dressed very quietly. By eight forty-five she was out the door for a little window-shopping.

When she returned an hour or so later, she found the bed unmade, the whiplash collar on the floor, and no Carl. She immediately ran to the front desk to ask the concierge if he had seen her husband. "Excuse me?" she said, and the cologne-doused concierge raised his head from beneath the souvenir counter. He seized her hand and began kissing it.

"*Vous êtes française?*" he crooned.

"No, I'm Ferguson in 309," she answered, all business.

"Oh, you are American! I am also to speak American also!" he said with a slight bow.

Dorothy opened her purse, removed a little cloth hankie with cats on it, and started to scrub her oversmooched hand. She came straight to the point. "Did you see a man leave here this morning without a whiplash collar?"

"I am sorry, but I am only to notice the ladies," he said, turning on all of his Latin charm.

"Thanks anyway," said Dorothy as she hurriedly reached into her purse and gave him a handful of lire worth about sixty dollars. "I'm sure he's all right."

Dorothy spent the entire morning canvassing the maze of Venetian walkways and waterways. No Carl. She checked the hotel again. No Carl. Finally she asked the concierge if there was a bar in Venice where people spoke English. He suggested that perhaps she meant Harry's Bar near the Grand Canal and offered to take her there. She declined, wiped her hand off again, and set out for Harry's. Two hours later she found the joint with the help of a very nice young Italian policeman who had learned English from Ricky Nelson records. "Be bop a lu la," he said as they parted ways.

It was two o'clock and packed at Harry's, but Dorothy was able to corner the barkeep long enough to extract the following information: a man who fit the description of Carl had in fact been in earlier that day. He had consumed several very dry Beefeater martinis and four complete bowls of Cheetos. The barkeep recalled him as moody and often given to talking to himself. He further recalled that, upon leaving, the man had said, "Next time around I'll just honk."

That was all Dorothy had to go on. She ordered a Pimm's Cup, sat down, and proceeded to rack her brains. For a fleeting moment she stared at the cheap paper coaster that said "HARRY'S" and thought about the nice ones with the little cats. But mostly her mind was on Carl.

Carl, meanwhile, was well outside of the Venice city limits in a little hamlet called Pittuli. Pittuli was the nearest town to Venice that had an Avis Rent A Car office. Carl was determined to get his money's worth.

Having selected a small yellow Fiat from the storage lot, Carl proceeded to the dispatcher with his prearranged contract and Visa card in hand.

Luigi, the dispatcher, was a little hesitant to release one of his brood without more documentation or an Avis charge card. After many minutes of awkward bilingual confrontation the problem was solved when Carl bellowed at the top of his lungs. "*Visa!* It's the same thing as *Avis!* It's a goddamned anagram for Christ's sake! Don't you greaseballs ever do the Jumble in the paper?"

Either Luigi was able to break through the language barrier and see the logic of Carl's remarks, or he was too tired to deal with another American lunatic. In any event, Carl was soon behind the wheel of the little yellow Fiat whizzing his way toward Venice.

Ordinarily, getting a car into the center of Venice is a job that should be undertaken only by the Seabees, trained mercenaries, or people who make television commercials. These, however, were not ordinary circumstances.

At the age of sixty-seven, Carl Ferguson was feeling something that few white men ever feel. He was feeling a purpose. He was going to be the first man to drive into Piazza San Marco. He felt like Columbus, John Glenn, and Bullitt all rolled into one.

Forcefully, if not skillfully, he guided his rapidly disintegrating Fiat down the little footpaths, over the stepstone bridges, and right through the chairs and tables of sidewalk cafés. He insured that no one would get hurt by keeping his hand on the horn the entire time.

Dorothy Ferguson had gone to the Bridge of

Sighs with a pair of binoculars to search for her husband. The binoculars were on loan from the concierge, who used them to check on "room occupancy." The first thing she noticed was an enormous cheering crowd entering the Piazza San Marco.

It seems that in a scant hour and a half, Carl's grinding and crunching his way through the streets of Venice had made him an instant folk hero for most of the population.

"*Andiamo!*" they cried. "*Andiamo!*"

Dorothy heard the horn blaring. It was the same blare she was used to back in Akron whenever there were chickens in the road. She feared the worst and ran for the Piazza.

When the roofless, hoodless, three-wheeled vehicle finally limped into San Marco, the crowd split and clung to the walks like preteens at a school dance. The only person left standing in San Marco Square was Dorothy Ferguson, and she was immobile and pissed to the limit.

It seemed like hours before the little yellow Fiat finally gouged its way to the center of the square, but it made it, stopping a mere two feet from where Dorothy was standing. The engine coughed its last, and Carl emerged to thunderous applause and cheering. Carl now added Rocky to the list of people he felt like. Carl ran to Dorothy, seeing her as Talia Shire. "Carl, you've ruined our vacation," she said. "And you should be wearing your collar." There was no embrace. Instead she turned and walked away straight through the throng of oncoming admirers.

Dorothy spent the next two heavily sedated days and nights at the Garibaldi Hotel as her husband began his mandatory three-month jail term as a public nuisance.

Suddenly, on the third morning, Dorothy awoke with her own sense of purpose. I've got to get on with my life, she said to herself. She promptly went downstairs and asked the concierge if he would be so kind as to quit his job immediately and escort her to Greece, and then back to America. The concierge fell to his knees and accepted with such profuse hand-kissing that he was nearly dehydrated. By two o'clock that afternoon they were on their way to Athens.

It was about a month into Carl's jail sentence that he received a visit from a young journalist with *People* magazine. Carl was very animated in his retelling of the incident, his arms flailing madly, as if he still had the wheel. It was right after he said, "I don't see how I could ever top it," that he inadvertently hit himself in the Adam's apple.

It was long after Carl's funeral, long after Dorothy closed up the Akron house, and long after the concierge stopped writing that Dorothy sat in the backyard of Gwennie's Ocala, Florida, home, staring at the sunset. She racked her brain once again as to what could have happened to the little glass unicorns. She remembered wrapping them in tissue paper, one by one, and tucking them into the big suitcase right between her hair spray and her travel-tips book. Somehow they had just disappeared.

3

Diary of a White Wedding

PREFACE

Diaries are hard to come by. You can either write one yourself or hope that someone in your family leaves his open by the nightstand. They are a potential embarrassment to anyone who keeps one. No one wants you to see his diary until he's dead and gone, or famous enough to have it published and pawn it off as a literary masterpiece, like Anaïs Nin.

We got lucky. We bought the following diary at a garage sale in Wheaton, Illinois. We stopped to look at the largest assortment of slightly bent TV trays we had ever seen, and instantly fell in love with this delightful little girl's diary, bound in an intricate Leatherette brocade and secured by the proverbial padlock. The people holding the sale had bought it at another garage sale, then lost the key to the lock, so it was worthless to them except as bookcase filler. They didn't think thirty-five cents was too much to ask, and neither did we. The padlock was a snap to break.

For easy reading, we chose the best parts and left out the interminable entries about Thanksgiving, Christmas, and the Super Bowl. Inspired by those letters they're always finding written by pioneer women in the middle of a horrible winter in the wilds of Montana, we homed in on the big issues of life: getting married and writing all those thank-you notes.

Sunday, June 4, 1978.

Dear Diary,
   Well, it finally happened! James Paul Rockerman 3rd, just about the sweetest, dearest, nicest man that ever walked the face of the earth, asked *me* to marry him! And I said yes! It's a dream come true! Now I don't have to worry about graduate school or getting my own apartment or anything! I can just move from the sorority house right into his place (where I've been sleeping most nights for the last three years anyway, but don't tell Mom and please don't tell his mom, she would absolutely kill me!). I just looooove his family. They're so much better than my family, it's scary! (Don't tell Mom that, either.) Anyway, his mom is so funny and treats me just like a real daughter, and his dad gave him a new car just for not flunking out and his younger brother is cuter than he is and I

could go on and on but I got a million things to do! I only have one year from today before the wedding! Will I ever get it all done? I doubt it!

Saturday night, September 16, 1978.

Dear Diary,

I hate Paulie's mother, I hate her with a passion! She has completely taken over *my* wedding and made my life miserable. First, she insisted that the ceremony be held in *her* Methodist church instead of our Methodist church because their pastor baptized Paulie and ours just moved here from Baton Rouge, Louisiana, and they have a bigger sanctuary for all of her 10,000 friends who I don't care if they come anyway! My dad was furious—he's paying for everything, you know—until he and Paulie's dad went out and played golf about a hundred times and decided to let the women fight it out. My mom gave in, of course. I think she's scared of Paulie's mom. They *did* let us ask my Sunday-school teacher, Mrs. Reynolds, to sing "I Believe" during the ceremony. It's my favorite wedding song and it turns out to be Paulie's mom's favorite too, so I guess there's still some hope for this family!

Right now I'm working on the invitations. My sister Margie helped for a while, but she got sick of writing with a quill pen and then she called Paulie's brother and they went out, which makes me sick, because she's just trying to

prove that I'm not the only one in this house
that's attractive to the Rockermans. Sometimes
she seems like my very best friend and then all
of a sudden she's like the Joan Collins of Kappa
Alpha Theta! Mom says Margie feels left out of
all the wedding hoopla. But how could she?
She's my first bridesmaid! And she's cute. She'll
find a husband someday, but probably not as
good as my Paulie!

Friday, January 12, 1979.

Dear Diary,
    For the very first time today, I had second
thoughts about marrying Paulie. First, I hate the
name Robin Rockerman. I always have, but
today it started to make me sick to my stomach!
And here's why. We had the whole Rockerman
family over tonight for dinner—Mom fixed her
famous Standing Pork Roast and Vegetables and
they seemed to enjoy it, except Paulie's hunk
brother Randy who thinks he can go to
Hollywood and be a stuntman after he
graduates in Physical Education next spring, so
he only ate a ton of scallop potatoes with his
shirt off. So, after dinner, I ran upstairs to put
on my wedding dress that I spent all week
hemming myself, and when I came down to
show everyone in the TV room, Paulie takes one
look and shouts out, "Who made that thing?
Miss Piggy of Paris!!" Everyone had a good

laugh except me, and even though Paulie said he was just kidding and I looked like an angel from heaven, I hated him so much I almost threw his cheap zircon ring in his face! I went through a hundred *Bride's* magazines finding this pattern by Harold of Milan and Mom spent six weeks making it! It's a good thing she was in the kitchen icing the Bundt cake or she would have been crushed! I'm gonna go out and buy a new one on Monday and not show it to that jerk Paulie until I'm coming down the aisle and it's too late!

Friday, January 26, 1979.

Dear Diary,

I got my very first wedding present today! A butter knife! It's so pretty! Everyone in the sorority just loved it when I showed it around at the Songfest. I called Paulie to tell him, but his Little Brother at the frat house said he was at the library studying for a test in his Biz Ad course, "Service After the Sale." Fat chance! He's probably out with that slut Mary Ann McEnnis! I don't really care, but don't tell him that. It makes me feel like a big shot and I know he loves me. I got the ring to prove it!

I just love our silverware pattern! It's kind of Danish and kind of old-fashioned at the same time. Good silverware is the most important thing you can get at a wedding, Mom says. That and guest towels. Did you know there are places where you can sell wedding presents you don't want? Who in the world would want to do that!?

Wednesday, March 21, 1979.

Dear Diary,
   Only 72 days left! I just can't wait. I know things will be a lot better between Paulie and me after we get married. We're back home for Easter break now, so we went to have a chat about God and sex and fidelity and stuff with Reverend Rodgers, the guy that's going to marry us, and Paulie was so rude! Every time Mr. Rodgers said something about the holy bliss of sexual union or coveting thy neighbor's wife, Paulie would pop up with, "No problem, Rev, my neighbor's wife is sixty years old and weighs two hundred pounds!" or "I know, Doc, I read all about it in the *Penthouse Forum*." Mr. Rodgers was very sweet, though. He kept holding my hand and calling me "child" and gave us a book called *The Joy of Methodist Sex* when we left. I'm halfway through already and have learned a lot.
   You know, you really find out stuff about your fiancé when you're about to get married to him. Paulie hates his mom, he told me the other day, and his dad, too, and his brother Randy and just about everyone except Mary Ann McEnnis, who he didn't mention at all, of course. He said his mom likes me "too much"! I said what is that

supposed to mean. He said his mom has been pushing him to marry me since his freshman year, that his mom wanted this marriage more than he did! That's when I really got upset, but I felt a lot better after he pulled out a present his aunt gave him to give to me. A soup ladle!

I'm not even sure that Paulie believes in God. Now wouldn't that be something!

Saturday, April 21, 1979.

Dear Diary,

Am I exhausted or what!!! Three bridal showers, a shoe fitting, an aerobics class, and a heart-to-heart talk with Paulie's mom, all in one day! Paulie went off rabbit hunting and beer-drinking with his friends, so he was no help, and the fact that I have to lose fourteen pounds in the next six weeks and haven't eaten anything but Jell-O and Lipton's Instant Ice Tea since last Tuesday makes my stomach growl while everyone else is stuffing theirs!

The shoe fitting went fine. The shoe man is going to stretch my grandmother's wedding shoes three and a half sizes so I have something "old" to wear on the big day. The first shower was a surprise shower at 6:30 AM, thrown by all my sorority sisters. It was like a stag party for girls. I turned over in my sleep and there was this male dancer from the nightclub "Girls Night Out" snuggled up beside me in bed wearing nothing but a little pouch! He started to

45

kiss me and put his hands you-know-where and
I just let him, even though my hair was in big
rollers and I only had on Paulie's "Property of
Beta Theta Pi" T-shirt. Just after he took the T-
shirt off and everything else, out jumped all my
sisters yelling "Surprise! Surprise! We're going
to tell Paulie!!" Boy was I surprised! Mr. Well-
Endowed left and we all laughed at the
Polaroids that Nancy Johnson took of the giant
grin on my face when he started to get on top.
They'll look great in the sorority scrapbook!

After Mom served up her famous Sara Lee
coffee cake and we sang songs and cried a lot,
they all left and I tried to figure who gave me
which teddy bear. Anyway, we barely had time
to dress for the big luncheon Mrs. Rockerman
(she wants me to call her either "Mom" or
"Sally," but I just can't) was throwing at her
house. Except for all the silverware I got, it was
awful! I thought my face was going to crack
from all that smiling, and I almost screamed the
five hundredth time one of those old bags said,
"Boy, you sure are lucky to have found a catch
like Paulie!" If you ask me, Paulie's the one that
ought to be counting his lucky stars!

After they left and my mom was doing the
dishes, "Sally" took me into her bedroom and
really got personal. First she asked me if I was a
virgin. I could have died! I lied and said yes, and
she said too bad, because Paulie doesn't know
shit about how to please a woman and that I
will have to teach him everything like a two-

year-old, just like she had to teach Buddy and he still hasn't caught on! That's when I told her that Paulie and I had done it probably a thousand times and that he was no better now than he was that first night on their living-room rug. We had a real chuckle over that, and then she gave me her favorite vibrator and insisted that I take it. It was sooo sweet!

Then she hit me with a real bombshell. *Paulie is not really a Rockerman!!!* Buddy is not his real dad and Randy is not his real brother! After I threw up all over her new bedspread, we pitched it into the bathtub and she explained the whole thing. Two weeks before she married Buddy, she completely fell for this jazz trumpet player that showed up out of the blue at the travel agency where she worked. His name was Zoot and he was from "Frisco." That's all she can remember about him. Anyway, she had nothing to do that night, what with Buddy working down at the ice plant (as usual), Zoot was lonely, and she needed the practice. Oh, what a night! To this day, every time she hears Doc Severinsen on TV, she cries a tear for Zoot.

Until that moment, she had never told anyone her little secret. *I was the first!* Buddy and Paulie think they're father and son, although they never really liked each other. Buddy thinks Paulie is lazy and a crybaby, and he's right, but at least now I know why! Sally says that if I can get Paulie to do exactly what I tell him to— which is really pretty easy, since she and Buddy

have been telling him what to do his whole
life—then he'll make a great husband and
maybe we'll have a son that's a famous jazz
musician. Now, that's something to look
forward to!

There's only one problem, Sally says. Getting
Paulie to the altar. Sure, he wants to get
married, but sometimes he cuts off his nose to
spite his face, she says. Like the time Buddy
made him go out for football in high school and
all of a sudden his appendix burst! Buddy made
him play anyway, stitches and all, but he was
never very good. So, if I can get that ring on his
finger, I'm home free!

Sally is really on top of things. Why can't my
mother be like that?

Thursday, May 3, 1979.

Dear Diary,

Boy, Mom hates Paulie's mom! She thinks
she's a phony and secretly despises and looks
down her nose at our whole family, except for
me, of course. She calls her "Queen Sally," as in,
"Are you sure that Queen Sally would approve
of a chartreuse tablecloth?" (She didn't.)
Apparently Sally said something nasty about
people who live in trailer parks and buy their
clothes at Monkey Wards at their bridge party
the other day, and Mom took it the wrong way, I
think. Sally knows we have to live like this
because of Dad's mood swings and not because

he doesn't want a steady job. I think it makes Mom nervous that Paulie's dad is loaning my dad the money to pay for the wedding. She should lighten up!!!

I finally finished *The Joy of Methodist Sex* and gave it to my sister but I can't lose weight! Yesterday I started throwing up even the Jell-O and ice tea after every meal, so maybe that will help. Paulie's dad keeps sneaking up behind me and putting his arms around my waist and saying I'm "plump for the picking." Mom loves it when he does that to her. I hate it!

Speaking of plump, you should see Paulie! He's starting to look like Dom De Luise and act like him too! He runs into the house, counts the toaster ovens and stuff on display in the living room, and takes off for another beer party without even a peck on the cheek or a "Who gave us the goat cheese and yogurt maker?" I wonder about that boy, I really do. Dad says I should worry if he *doesn't* get drunk every night before the wedding! I know, I know, I saw the movie *Bachelor Party*, but it still worries me. I'm sure he'll settle down after we get married and his dad gets him a good job in the carpet business, maybe his own outlet!

Sunday, May 20, 1979.

Dear Diary,

I'm so scared! Fourteen days from today I will be walking down the aisle a married woman

and what if it isn't just perfect? What if it's a
dud, like a bad Super Bowl game or the time
Paulie and I spent over a $100 to go see Simon
and Garfunkel in concert and I swear that
Garfunkel was spaced out or maybe just mad at
Simon and they sang five or six songs and left
and Paulie and I had the biggest fight of our life
on the way home in his car. Paulie said that
Simon and Garfunkel were stupid and it really
made me furious!

But not as furious as yesterday! Yesterday
really took the cake. Sally Rockerman called
this big meeting of both families to go over
every last detail of both the wedding and the
reception. Mom got all huffy on the way over,
saying that if Queen Sally ordered her to do one
more thing she would tell her to go straight to,
but of course she didn't. She just smiled and
smoked cigarettes like always.

Sally had these huge seating charts set up in
her living room and really made it sound like a
big society wedding! First, everybody would get
an "I Believe" button as they came into the
church, to go with the song and everything.
Then after they're seated and can see themselves
on the closed-circuit TV sets that Reverend
Rodgers will set up, Paulie and his twelve Best
Men come out in their matching white tuxedos
and red silk scarves. Each one then steps up to
the microphone and finishes the sentence,
"When I think of Paulie and Robin, I think of the
time . . ." God, I hope Chuck Sturges doesn't

talk about the time Paulie brought me upstairs drunk as a skunk to the third-floor "Playboy Mansion" room at the Beta House at three in the morning! He wouldn't, would he? I better call him.

Anyway, after that, the horn players come out and play the fanfare from "Hail to the Chief." Everybody turns and I make my grand entry, riding in one of those Cinderella pumpkin coaches carried on big wooden shafts by six guys that work down at Buddy's carpet store. They have on white tuxedos, too. In front of us are my twelve bridesmaids, of course, including my cousin Bethie, who I hate, and they're tossing little crepe paper poppies into the pews as they walk, and behind them are those adorable little two-year-olds, Sean and Dawn, carrying the ring on a big satin pillow. Dad brings up the rear. The tough part for me is getting out of the coach at the altar without tripping on my train or something. I'll be so weak from not eating by then, anything could happen!

The ceremony will be real simple. Reverend Rodgers will do his "We're gathered here together" speech and then Paulie and I take over. We not only made up our own vows, we made up our own service! First we introduce our moms and dads to everyone in the church and give them a big hand. Then we show our own baby pictures on the TV monitors. Then all my sorority sisters stand up and sing "My Guy."

Then we say our vows. Paulie is going to read a passage from one of Dr. Robert Schuller's *Hour of Power* sermons that talks about marriage as the longest-running TV show of your whole life (and you're writing the scripts!). I'm going to say this:

"Paulie, you are my man, now and forever. You are the sunshine of my life and there will never be a cloud of doubt in my mind to dampen your warm glow. I know you will work hard to provide for our family. Even if you fail, you will never lose your sense of humor and neither will I. I'm sure you will find something to do with your life. Almost everybody does. If not, I'll be the family breadwinner myself. I will also be the mother of your children, two boys, two girls, Paulie Junior, Buddy Junior, Robin Ann, and little Princess Sally, and a loyal sexual, spiritual, and traveling companion, always. Before God, Reverend Rodgers, and all these wonderful friends and family of ours, I now pronounce myself Mrs. James Paul Rockerman the 3rd, your wife for life."

Then Mrs. Reynolds sings "I Believe," everybody cries, and we head for the reception. That's the plan. This is where Sally got real excited. She loves receptions! She had barely gotten started on the nut cups when into the room stumbles Paulie and my dad, both too drunk for words! Paulie made a joke about saving a bundle by driving to Vegas and getting it over with and my dad started laughing like a hyena. You could have heard a pin drop in that room when he stopped. They left to get more beer, Sally said she was tired of talking and just handed out Xerox seating assignments for the reception, and we all ate chili and went home.

Mom called Rawley Hills that night about Paulie's drinking problem and they said don't do anything until after the wedding. I hope they're right!

Friday, June 1, 1979.

Dear Diary,

Guess what? Not more than two hours ago, Paulie Rockerman ruined my life! I'm not kidding. *The wedding is off!!!!* Can you believe it? I can't.

Here's what happened. We were at the dress rehearsal tonight and everybody seemed to be having a great time, including Paulie. He was drunk, of course, but so were all of his Best Men, so no one really noticed. I was a little tipsy myself, I have to admit. You have to be to get up in one of those ridiculous hand-carried rickshas!

The baby picture and "My Guy" parts worked great and then it was time for Paulie's vows. Just when he got to the part where Reverend Schuller talks about "love as a story line that never wears thin," he stopped and looked at me and said, "Robin, you're a real sharp gal and one day you'll make some lucky guy a hell of a wife, but not me." I started laughing! I thought it was one of Paulie's last-minute jokes! So did everyone else, including his mom and dad.

That's when he really got upset.

"Listen," he started shouting, "I know what you're all thinking. You're thinking, What a royal fuck-up! What a jerk! What a complete embarrassment to the human race and the good name of Rockerman. None of you think I will ever, in a million years, amount to jack shit. I'm just happy-go-lucky Paulie, an amiable clodhopper that you can just order around. 'Paulie, don't drink! Paulie, don't gulp your food! Paulie, grow up!' Mother, I guess you got tired of me, so you're pawning me off on Robin. At least you get a respectable daughter-in-law in the trade. Well, I'm fed up with it, do you hear?

"I don't want to get married, I don't want to go into the carpet business, and I hope I never see another toaster oven as long as I live! From this moment on, *I'm going to do what I want!* I'm going to move to San Francisco and get a job as a longshoreman and learn to play the trumpet! I know that may come as a shock to you people, but I feel it in my blood. Call me a dreamer, call me a drifter, call me anything you want. But that's *the real me, the real PAUL*, not this mama's boy standing here, shaking in his boots. And I'm taking Mary Ann McEnnis with me!"

With that he stomped out of the church. No one else made a move. We were all too stunned. I didn't even cry. In my heart, I guess, I knew he was right. I *didn't* think he would ever amount to jack shit.

Monday, June 2, 1980.

Dear Diary,

I can't believe I haven't written in here in over a year! I guess I've just been too busy for words. I'll try to do better from now on.

Where do I start? Did I tell you about the wedding? Well, we didn't have one. We eloped instead. Paulie got sick of San Francisco and Mary Ann McEnnis and the life of a beginning trumpet student about three weeks after he walked out on me, so he snuck back into town and woke me up at three in the morning to apologize. Of course we had already sent all the presents back and eaten most of the food, so a new wedding was out of the question. Queen Sally wanted me to sue him for breach of contract, but I talked her out of it.

Paulie got a job—on his own!—as an ad salesman for a local radio station, so he can still pursue his interest in music. His brother Randy married my sister Margie, *of course*, and they moved to Hollywood to work for Lee Majors, and Queen Sally started her own wedding-planning business. She is such a dynamo!

All in all, I'm kind of glad it turned out this way. I was worried that my life was going to seem drab after such a big wedding, and now the wedding seems drab after such a big life! And I married a man instead of a mouse.

4

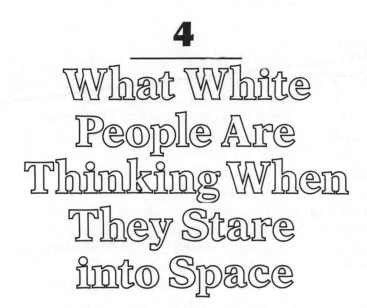

What White People Are Thinking When They Stare into Space

It is a popular misconception that white people are not thinking when they stare blankly into space. Given the myriad opportunities for blank staring that crop up every day in an average white person's life, the need for thinking about something becomes essential. The technical definition of "brain-dead" is too amorphous to run the risk of not having at least a thought or two.

Forrest Bender drove his Oldsmobile to the car wash. He pulled it up to the gas pumps, checked the glove compartment and trunk for valuables, and handed the keys over to the Filipino in the orange jumpsuit. He paid for his gas, car wash, and Carnuba wax job with his MasterCard and went outside to wait. They had little benches for that. Forrest knew that he had a good ten minutes for some serious staring into space.

Christ, what was it that Doris asked me to pick up? he began. I should've written it down. It was two things. One of them was probably bread and . . . yes, one of them was definitely a loaf of bread. It'll come to me. I wonder how they make anything at all on a four-dollar Carnuba waxing. Maybe it's not real Carnuba wax. Half of these little orange paratroopers look like they're probably *from* someplace named Carnuba. That must be how they get away with calling it Carnuba waxing. They probably just use watered-down Mop & Glow. Not a bad little racket when you think about it. These guys get to hang out with their fellow Carnubans all day long; more than likely they share one room somewhere at night. Send their paychecks home to Carnuba, never paying a dime of tax, and live off the tips. Ten years later they go back home to a nice little nest egg and spend the rest of their days riding donkeys and drinking beer. Meanwhile they get to drive nice-looking American cars, even if it's only for a few feet. What made me think of Mop & Glow a second ago? Was that the other thing on the list? No. Doris uses something else. Maybe she should try Mop & Glow. That floor never looks good. An air hammer, that's what that floor could use. Just tear up the damn thing and put down new linoleum. I should put Dave on that. Twenty-eight years old and still living at home; he should do something to pull his weight. Six weeks away from finishing dental school and he quits because that idiot girlfriend of his doesn't like the way it makes his hands smell. Two months later she runs off with a sportswriter from Utah. Probably one of those Mormons. Boy, I don't see how anyone can live without coffee. Was it coffee? No, we've got plenty of coffee. Maybe just put that new indoor-outdoor carpeting right over the old floor. At least it's cushioned. And I won't have to listen to Doris talking about her hip pains all day long. Burt has some in his garage. I should call him and find out what it ran him per foot. That Buick was two cars behind me and he's out first? Maybe he didn't have the Carnuba treatment.

Look at that license-plate holder. "IRV WINKLEMAN BUICK." You finally get enough money together to buy yourself respectable transportation and some car dealer has to plaster his name all over the rear end. They're not doing his side mirrors. They better do mine. Look at that—he's getting into his car anyway with the side mirrors still soapy. He gave the guy a dollar. Christ, I was going to go for fifty cents. Maybe the next guy won't give him anything and then my fifty cents will look pretty good. Here comes his wife, eating a Zag-Nut bar. That's the last thing she needs. She's got a butt on her like a sumo wrestler. Dave should go on a diet, too. I don't see how a grown man can respect himself watching game shows all day. What was that question on *Jeopardy* the other night that he knew and nobody else did? Something about Hoover Dam. The girl got it wrong and Dave got it right. Twenty thousand bucks and Dave could have won it. Maybe Doris should call her sister in California and see if they can't get Dave on one of those shows. *The $100,000 Pyramid* and the final category is Things a Guy Who Drops Out of Dental School Does. Dave and Florence Henderson. She'd give and he'd receive. He'd have enough money to hire someone to put in linoleum. Maybe treat his folks to a couple of weeks on the beach in Carnuba. Here comes the Olds. Boy, she looks good when she's wet. It just goes to show you, you take care of them and they'll take care of you.

———

Forrest checked his pocket to make sure that he had two quarters for the Carnuban and sauntered to his car. He pointed to the side mirrors and the young man redid them. Satisfied with the job and the tip, Forrest drove away to the A & P, where he purchased a loaf of sliced sandwich bread. On his way home he got stuck behind a funeral and once again had to stare into space for a few minutes.

He thought about the first car he ever owned and how he and Doris used to wash it themselves. He thought about Hoover Dam and the pretty black girl in the bread department at the A & P, and he wondered how many fifty-cent tips it would take to add up to what he took home in a week. It wasn't until he got halfway up the driveway to his house that he remembered that the other item was Drano.

5

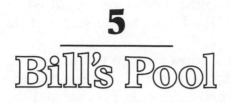

The Baltimore sun can play tricks on you, especially in the months of July and August. Bill hated the so called dog days of summer. He was a heavyset man and sweated profusely—maybe that had something to do with it. In any case, from the time he was a small boy watching *Flipper* on TV, he dreamed of having his own swimming pool to wallow around in whenever the mercury got over sixty-five degrees.

Bill liked to stay cool. He had the first central air-conditioning system on the block and drove a convertible with the AC on full blast. He carried around a battery-operated fan to cool himself off at the Orioles games. People clamored to sit behind him to catch the breeze.

Bill kept himself relatively dry eleven months out of the year. But August was always a cruel month and the reason most people move from Baltimore. Bill didn't have that luxury. He'd signed a thirty-year lease on his house that he planned to pay off before he went anywhere, and Baltimore was about the only place he could find work in the frozen crab cake business. He knew a good claw-and-pincer man could go broke quick in a place like Utah. So he suffered. Boy, did he suffer.

"Honey, I know we can't afford it, but this year I'm putting in a pool," he exclaimed one night over creamed crab cakes on toast.

"The hell you are, Bill Miller," his wife shot back. "There are a lot of things we need more than a pool for you to soak your fat ass in."

"But it's for your fat ass, too, honey. And there's nothing we need more than a pool," he rejoined.

"You got a minute? What about a garage-door opener so I don't have to throw my back out every time I bring home groceries? What about a living-room carpet that you can't see through? What about that trip to Atlanta to visit my mother that you've been promising for years? Bill, we don't need a pool."

"Alice, I don't like to pull rank at moments like these, but who brings home the crab cakes around here? Certainly not your mother. We're building a pool this year and that's that."

Bill left the table knowing he would not be sweating excessively from too much sexual activity in the next several months. But it was worth it. He'd put his foot down and his dream was close at hand. He could feel his fat ass cooling already.

Step one. Find a dependable and reasonable contractor. There were only four in Baltimore and he talked to all of them. He ended up with a firm called Can You Dig It.

Mr. Wilkins, president of Can You Dig It, came to see Bill's house personally to survey the backyard and explained the six pool models they had to choose from—kidney, oval, round, square, oblong, and "lake-like." Alice, apparently won over by Mr. Wilkins's easy charm, opted for "lake-like."

"It's two hundred dollars more than oblong," Bill complained. "It's not the rocks that cool you off, it's the water."

"It's our most popular model," Mr. Wilkins replied.

"Sold," said Alice, and the deal was consummated. Eleven hundred dollars, including lights and labor, no diving board. Total construction time: three days. Later that same evening, his life savings on the line, Bill lay awake in bed, wondering to himself, How in the hell can they build a "lake-like" pool in three days?

At six o'clock on Monday morning Bill got his answer. Dynamite went off in his backyard, blowing out two of the veranda windows and sending Alice's geraniums into orbit. "What the hell was that?" said Alice.

"That's step two, honey," Bill replied. "Digging the hole."

They both moved downstairs to inspect the damage. Looking through one of the broken window panes, Bill saw what looked like forty to forty-five black men with picks and shovels busily strip-mining the center of his backyard. "Why are they all wearing blue denim overalls and all chained together?" Alice wondered aloud.

Bill put his arm around her. "It's probably a union thing, honey, and if all that singing is any indication, they love their work. I wouldn't be surprised if they were finished in *two* days."

Bill was right. They *were* finished in two days. "Lake-like" turned out to be more lake-like than he ever imagined. All he bought was a big irregular hole in the backyard with a Styrofoam boulder at either end.

"You don't have to say it, Mr. Miller," said the unchained man with the shotgun, apparently the foreman. "I know what you're thinking. It looks like shit now, but wait till that sucker's filled with water. You'll blink your eyes and think you're in Vermont."

"Well, let's fill it," Bill exclaimed.

"Be happy to, Mr. Miller," said the foreman. "But of course that's another three hundred dollars. I'd have to free up one of the trustees and have him stand here for two days with a garden hose. And that means another hundred and fifty for someone to guard him."

"Is that a union regulation?" asked Bill.

"You could say that. The man might decide to hang himself with that garden hose and I'd be up shit's creek and you'd be liable. Neither of us want that. So that makes it four hundred and fifty dollars."

"Four hundred and fifty dollars?" moaned Bill. "And it's my water? My hose?"

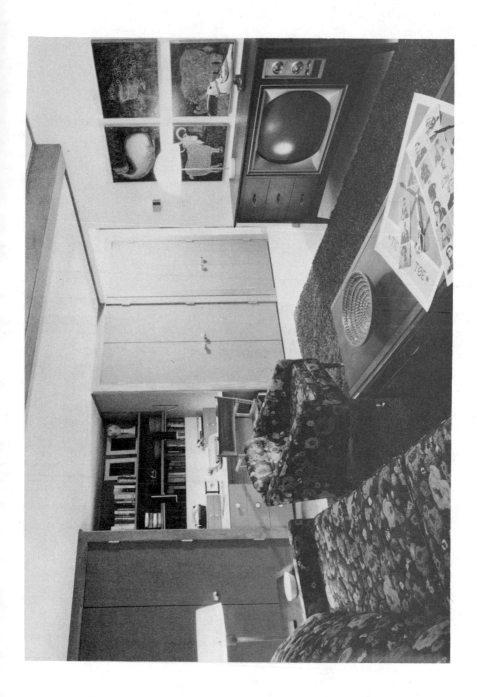

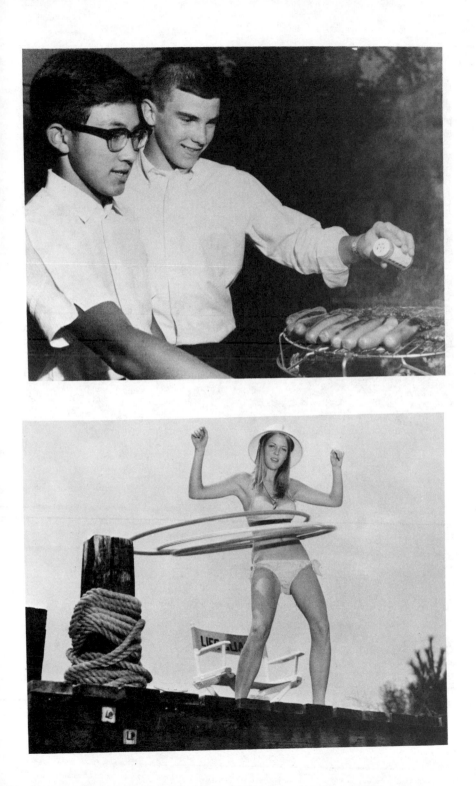

"I like you, Bill. I'll tell you what I'll do. You guard him yourself and I'll make it two hundred bucks, flat. You pay me now, cash."

"Fair enough," said Bill. It was a good thing that Bill had some vacation time coming, because it took four days to fill the pool instead of two. The water kept soaking into the ground.

On the third day Alice came out of the house at four in the morning to check on Bill. "What do you think, honey? It's looking more and more like Vermont, isn't it?" said Bill.

"Yes it is, sweetheart, but the front yard is starting to look like Louisiana during the rainy season. You could grow rice out there."

Bill had apparently flooded the neighborhood and the "lake-like" pool was still only two feet deep. He turned off the hose, put the trustee up in the extra bed in the attic, locked the door, and first thing the next morning called Mr. Wilkins. "We got us a problem here."

Mr. Wilkins arrived late that afternoon, released the trustee on his own recognizance, and sat down at the kitchen table with the Millers.

"I've been in the swimming pool business over twenty years, and this pops up every now and again," he explained. "I'm not a bit surprised. The bottom line is: Baltimore likes 'lake-like,' but 'lake-like' doesn't like Baltimore. It's like cabbage with a lot of you white people."

"Well, what do we do?" asked Alice.

"Stay away from cabbage!"

"We already do, Mr. Wilkins," Bill said. "Now back to the pool. What are our options?"

"Well, there are only two options, Mr. Miller, and both are gonna cost you some money. Option number one. Fill it back up with the original dirt. It's still in your garage. We always do that on a 'lake-like,' just in case this happens."

"Option number two. Sell your house to me. Let's face it: right now you don't want it and no one else does either, not with that godawful mud hole in the backyard. I'm prepared to give you ten thousand dollars cash."

Bill was stunned. "You gotta be kidding. This home, especially with a pool, is worth a hundred and ten thousand!"

"But the place doesn't have a pool, Miller, it has a mud hole. Ten thousand. Take it or leave it."

"Isn't there anything else we can do?" chimed in Alice.

"Well, now that you mention it, there is one last option. Line it with redwood. We had a couple up at Wilmington who did that to their 'lake-like' and it came out real nice."

"What does something like that run?" Bill asked.

"Well, it's four dollars a board-foot, not counting labor, and you've got a huge hole back there. I don't have my calculator with me. Let's just say, it's gonna set you back for the rest of your life. Interested?"

Bill left the room to get a towel and came back. "No can do, Mr. Wilkins. Redwood is out. I'm not a rich man," he said. "What now?"

"Well, Bill, I've held up my end of the bargain and threw in a free house call to boot. The ball's in your court. If I were you, I'd go down to the library, pick up a couple of books on swimming-pool construction, and do it yourself."

Bill stood up from the table, smiling. "That's exactly what I'll do, Mr. Wilkins, and I can't thank you enough for all your help. I just hope I get it done before August."

Bill was first in line at the local branch library the next morning and checked out the following books: *So You Want to Build a Pool?*, *Concrete and You*, *Lakes of Vermont*, and *Water Tables of Central Maryland*. By the time he had digested the contents of all four August was fast approaching.

Bill knew he had to turn on the steam. He took all the vacation time he'd ever built up plus enough sick leave for open-heart surgery and applied himself to the task. He bought acres of wire mesh, his own cement mixer, four tons of gravel, and five more Styrofoam boulders. He taught Alice how to mix the mud and slap it on. They worked day and night and were never closer. Alice had her mother flown in from Atlanta, and she pitched in as well. Her specialty was the little Mexican tile trim.

By two PM on August first, the pool was already filling. Bill was dragging more hose from the front yard to the back when a man in a cheap khaki suit holding a clipboard approached him. He showed him a badge that read BUILDING IN-SPECTOR.

"Bill Miller?" he asked.

"Yes," said Bill.

"Do you have a pool?" he asked.

"Yes, sir, we do," Bill said beaming.

"No, sir, you don't," the man said. "Not in this neighborhood. Not without a permit."

Bill didn't seem too dejected when the inspector told him he had broken every building ordinance in the city code and would have to return his backyard to its former state or face two years in a correctional institution. Bill had only one request. "Can I swim in it once?"

"Certainly," the inspector said, and joined him for a long dip in the hot August sun. Alice and Mom wore their new bikinis. Everyone had a wonderful time.

The next morning Bill and Alice started the laborious task of hauling the dirt from the garage and filling in their masterpiece.

Four months later, antsy to create something else, they sold their house and bought a small piece of property in Vermont. There was no lake on it but Bill and Alice knew they could build one!

6

Murder on the Block

Alice Fox was convinced that her next-door neighbor really was a threat to mankind, and she was going to do something about it. This had bothered her for years. Her husband Carl, of course, knew nothing about her suspicions. She wasn't about to expose herself to his heartless ribbing about her fantasy life. She loved fantasies, especially Harlequin ones, and he teased her about it every time he picked up one of her cherished, well-thumbed copies of *Stranger in the Bush* or *The Chateau of Eternal Desire* that she kept neatly boxed and catalogued under the daybed in the sewing room. And the kids, well, the kids just thought the neighbors were mindless dolts like everyone else that lived in this godforsaken Duckburg. But Alice knew. Fifteen years as recording secretary and volunteer organizer of the "Help a Kid, Help a Nation" counseling program at the Jaycees Auxiliary had taught her a thing or two about human nature. She knew there were some fish to fry down at 1633.

She had not liked Pam Adams from the moment she first laid eyes on her. Pam was cold. Smiling for her was a concerted effort. She seemed to mock every gesture of friendship and neighborliness that Alice could muster, and Alice was not one easily discouraged from the task of making someone feel like one of the family. "We like you whether you like it or not!" was Alice's lifelong motto—she put it on T-shirts, barbecue aprons, kitchen "To Do" pads, even a special-order throw rug for the family room—and it worked ninety-nine times out of a hundred. It worked with troubled teens, nasty washing-machine repairmen, the terminally ill at County Hospital, and as far as Alice was concerned, probably the Russians. But not Pam Adams. I don't like her and she likes it that I don't like her, Alice often pondered. It was completely baffling. That woman needs professional help, she concluded.

Her first theory was that Pam drank constantly and invited teenage boys over when her husband was gone and danced around the veranda with tassels on her tits and only a boa for a bottom. Her husband was gone a lot—he sold computers or something and didn't seem to have much of a future. Anyway, this scenario came to Alice in a dream. "Trust your dreams. They're trying to tell you something you don't want to hear." Alice couldn't remember where she picked that up, probably on TV, but it always worked for her.

It took her six months to give up on that particular hunch. Every day after school she trained her binoculars on the Adamses' veranda—she pretended to be bird-watching in the backyard—and never once caught "the dance of the seven veils," as she called it. She interrogated every teenage boy in the neighborhood, including her own, and none would confess to witnessing this scandal or even knowing Pam Adams, which proved nothing to Alice, who had long been convinced that all teenage boys were both pathological liars and sexual deviants. But she did start having second thoughts about the theory after going through the Adamses' garbage night after night. They ate a lot of frozen pizzas and bought only plain-wrap paper products, but she could find no used boas and no evidence of alcohol abuse. If they drank, they stored the bottles in the basement.

It was back to square one for Alice. She kept looking for a new dream to follow, but nothing new came, just the same lifelong nightmare of waking up and weighing three hundred pounds and having Carl come home and announce that he had lost all their money in a football pool and had never loved her anyway and was running off to Hawaii with a nineteen-year-old dental assistant. The hardest thing for Alice, of course, was going it alone. She needed someone to bounce her ideas off, help her collect evidence, and then share the supreme joy of nailing Pam

Adams. Thank God Chuck Dorran lived across the street. If he hadn't gotten sacked down at Imperial Life or, as he put it, "taken an early retirement to try my hand at plywood household accessories," Alice would have been lost.

Then there was the problem of Dad. Dad was Carl's eighty-three-year-old father, Carl Fox, Sr., a retired dentist who had lived in the guestroom off the kitchen since his wife died nine years ago. Dad was not much of a bother—he preferred to stay in his room and listen to call-in radio shows all day. But sometimes between callers he'd come wandering out looking for someone to argue with about the rights of Soviet Jews, and Alice would have to stop her menu planning and listen. After about an hour and a half of this, she'd finally shout, "Dad, I don't care if Chad falls into the hands of the Libyans, I got a family to feed," and he'd wander back into his room, shaking his finger at the wall, and stay there until the evening news.

Chuck Dorran's idea was to let Dad in on the investigation, but Alice knew he would soon forget the oath of secrecy and blurt out the lurid details at the dinner table. No, she would constantly have to wear a Walkman tuned to Dad's favorite station and dash back home every time the call-in subject changed in order to meet Dad storming out of his room. Of course, if they were poring over leads at Alice's house instead of Chuck's, she would have to send Chuck into the utility room when Dad was "out" to avoid the obvious question: "What in the hell is he doing here in the middle of the day?" It was a big hassle, but if it meant closing the door on that despicable Pam Adams, it was worth it.

Chuck was a great asset. Like Greg Morris on the old *Mission: Impossible*, he was a whiz with the technical stuff and had the kind of everyday looks that fit perfectly into a fake gas-company uniform or behind the wheel of a diaper-service Econoline van. Alice thought he was one of life's thrill seekers, a rare breed on her block. She knew she could never walk up to someone's front door and start ranting like a Jehovah's Witness just to see what the lady of the house was wearing at nine in the morning. Chuck could do it without blinking. She wondered why he never married, but was afraid to ask. He might have some incurable disease she didn't want to know about.

Chuck went after the Adamses' case with both barrels. He steamed open their mail on a daily basis. He tapped their phone and stuck a miniature microphone on their bedroom window to record their lovemaking. This was enjoyable to listen to, Alice concluded, but didn't provide much in the way of solid evidence. Posing as a bank loan officer, he went through their credit file at TRW for the last twenty years. Except for a lapsed subscription to *Child Love* magazine, which Alice thought must be akin to *Boys' Life* or *Family Circle*, they found little there they could use.

Nevertheless they pressed on. Chuck was offered another job in the insurance business, as a claims adjuster specializing in convenience-store robberies, but he turned it down flat. Alice dropped out of the Jaycees Auxiliary, bought a police-band radio, and attended every criminal trial in a radius of five hundred miles looking for a new angle. Dad seemed to accept her explanation that there was an outbreak of cholera among her friends and they needed her constant attention, although he never heard anything about it on the call-in shows.

In fact, Dad was elaborating on this in some detail to Alice one day when Chuck, sitting on a family-sized box of Tide in the utility closet, had a brainstorm and cracked the Adams case wide open. It was about time; Alice had grown despondent and was about ready to call in the police. According to Chuck, Pam Adams had murdered her husband months if not years ago, had cut him up into frozen pizzas that she kept discarding, piecemeal and partially eaten, in the family trash, and that the man we all thought was Walt Adams, her husband, was actually one of the local teenagers dressed to look much older. Alice bought it immediately. It all fit. The initial cold shoulder. The big freezer in the garage. *Child Love* magazine. The elaborate "I love you, dear" and "I missed you, dear" ceremonies at the front door every time "Walt" took off or came back from a business trip. All they needed now was the "smoking gun," one piece of incontrovertible proof, and *60 Minutes* would be pounding down the door.

Alice was so excited that hubby Carl thought she had been drinking sherry before dinner. Later that same evening he figured it was a good time to make his monthly move, but as usual she sidestepped his advances with the ironclad excuse that Dad would wake up from all the noise, begin to think about Mom, and not come out of his room for days. In any case, tonight she could not be distracted. Tomorrow she and Chuck were going in for the kill.

Every Thursday Pam Adams got her hair done. She left at precisely 11:30 AM and returned promptly at 2:45 in the afternoon. Chuck concluded that they had to get inside that house and find something of Walt's, like his wedding ring or AAA card, that he wouldn't leave behind while on "a business trip," unless that business was a trip to the afterlife. That, and a sample from one of the pizzas, would give them an airtight case.

At 11:15, Chuck knocked on Alice's back door, pretending to borrow some Cool Whip, their usual ploy. Dad was just summing up U.S. policy in Sri Lanka and rushing back to join the radio discussion on "Laughing Your Way Out of Terminal Cancer," so he just brushed Chuck off with a cursory "Why don't you get a job?" As soon as his door was shut, they were tiptoeing across the backyard, headed toward their rendezvous with homicide. They were dressed like city trash collectors to avoid suspicion. Only a shrewd onlooker would notice that Alice was taking Polaroids every step of the way.

Chuck stood watch while Alice, her heart racing, slipped in through the sliding glass veranda doors. She was absolutely electrified with fear. She only came close to being this excited once in her life, the time she almost took off all her clothes in front of Carl and Bill and Jenny playing strip poker. After retreating twice—each time Chuck shoved her back into the house—she headed up the stairs to the master bedroom. God, this is thrilling! she kept repeating to herself. I'll know every intimate detail about Pam Adams when this is over.

Pam Adams sure had her share of trashy lingerie. That's the first thing Alice noted as she rifled through her drawers. Teddies, push-up bras, a couple of merry widows. But where are the real garments? she wondered. And where is Walt's AAA card? In fact, where is anything of Walt's? This is all girl's stuff! There's not a black stretch sock or a boxer short to be seen.

She almost screamed with glee. Her mind was racing. That's it! Walt *must* be dead and cut into pizza parts, because she has destroyed any trace that he even lived here! If a man was on a business trip, he wouldn't take every shred of clothing! She burned his clothes because she didn't want to be reminded of her awful deed, and I got the Polaroids to prove it.

Alice was taking page-by-page photos of Pam Adams's diary on the nightstand when she heard something and turned. Her heart stopped. There before her stood Pam Adams herself, hands defiantly on her hips, her hair newly permed. "What in the hell are you doing here?" she said in a low, threatening, almost masculine voice.

"I'm here because you murdered your husband and burned all of his clothes," Alice barked back, surprised at her own assertiveness. "I'm gonna see you hang for this, bitch."

Alice then noticed that Pam was holding a tire iron, and knew she had to act quickly if she was going to live to tell about it. She lunged for the weapon but missed, and before she knew it Pam had her pinned to the ground and was sitting on her. Alice was helpless and Pam knew it. Pam started laughing a mad, undulating cackle that seemed surprisingly baritone for a middle-aged woman. Alice started whimpering and then suddenly, swish! she instinctively reached up and grabbed Pam's hair, and it came off in her hands! It was *Chuck* dressed up in women's clothes! Chuck was Pam! She gasped and fainted.

For some reason, when she came to, she had sense enough not to open her eyes. She laid there on Pam's bed, listening to Chuck talk to himself, confessing his vile deeds over and over again. "I had to kill her. She laughed at me when I told her I loved her and wanted to become her sex slave. When you, Alice, suspected something, I knew I had to play along or be found out. And once we were seen together by your Dad, I knew I could implicate you in the murder and shut you up.

But, now, I have the overwhelming urge to kill you too and make a convenience food out of you, so I *must* . . ."

Alice's hand reached the tire iron on the bed before Chuck's did, and with a force she didn't know she had, she whapped Chuck once and he was dead as a doornail. She held her tears inside, ran home to talk cancer with Dad for fifteen minutes, and then rushed back. What could she do? If she called the police, how would it look? They would conclude that she and Chuck were engaged in some bizarre sex ritual in Pam Adams's bedroom, that together they killed Pam, and then she killed Chuck. She could never live this one down!

Alice was nobody's fool. Her mother had always told her that, and for once she was right. Like in one of her dreams, Alice saw the whole scenario in a flash and executed it masterfully. First she disposed of Chuck with a method she doesn't like to recall, cleaned up the spot on the rug where he died, and tossed out the rest of the pizza. Upon discovering that Walt had his own bedroom and plenty of spare clothing, she located the Holiday Inn where he was staying in Portland and, imitating Pam's voice, demanded an immediate divorce and told him not to come home. She boxed up his clothes and shipped them to Portland, locked up the house, and took off for a fat farm for six weeks.

Dad's theory was that Alice and Chuck Dorran had run off together and were probably living it up in Brazil right now, and his many accounts of their sneaking around at all hours of the day and night made a pretty convincing case. "It's part of a bizarre sex ritual," Dad pronounced. "It's the number-one topic on talk radio." Carl never thought Alice loved him anyway and soon found someone to mend his broken heart at a Parents Without Partners meeting. The kids thought it was great that their mom had finally lived out one of her Harlequin fantasies, and when they got a loving postcard marked Rosarita, Mexico, they were very proud.

Meanwhile, Alice completely transformed herself into a clone of Pam Adams. She lost forty pounds, had her breasts enlarged, her face lifted, and her hair dyed, and with the generous divorce settlement, took up residence two doors down from her old life. She is *the* party giver on the block and is rumored to have had a number of affairs with married men, including Carl Fox. She never bought another frozen pizza.

7

A Big Day for Herb and Peggy

Rain like you wouldn't believe. Great for the farmer; living hell for the Olsens. All of the planning, all of the preparation, all of the hours spent making the little paper-bag Japanese lanterns. And now rain. It was as if God didn't care about all Peggy Olsen's hard work.

There's no way they can all fit in the house, Peggy thought to herself. Maybe I could have them come in shifts, but then that would ruin the surprise. There was really nothing to do except pray to God for nice weather tomorrow. Peggy crawled into bed, gently removed her pillow from under Herbert's arm, and silently prayed for nice weather. She prayed to the same God that, only moments before, she had accused of not caring about her party. It was the only God she knew.

Peggy had planned this get-together more for her mother than anyone else. Her father might well end up the life of the party—he usually did—but it would give her mother something to talk about for a long time to come. Fifty years of marriage should not go unnoticed. It should be celebrated, regaled, and saluted. Peggy took the entire chore upon herself with a happy heart. She collected and reglued dozens of dog-eared photo albums. She hand-planted rows of marigolds around the shed so that people "might want to sit back there." She made potato salad, macaroni salad, rice-and-raisin salad, tossed salad, her own special weiner-and-cold-cut salad, and enough fruit salad to end world hunger. She bought decorator Kleenex boxes for both bath rooms, bug bulbs for the patio "in case it went late," and actually swept the lawn with a broom.

Peggy knew she had held up her end. Still, though a good night's sleep was more than called for, she stared at the moon shadows on the drapes and wondered if the others had done the same. Frances won't be a problem, she thought to herself. She's been making those cheese balls for twenty years. Uncle Buddy might be a problem. Buddy was in charge of all of the beer and wine, or "hooch," as he liked to call it. Uncle Buddy was never more than three feet from a "gentleman's libation," so he knew his brand names and seemed like the perfect man for the job.

"Don't worry about the 'garni,'" her sister Helen told her over the phone. "It'll be there and crisp as a new dollar bill. I had Jack go buy one of those coolers."

Jack would be in charge of all of the barbecue. Jack had, over the years, come up with a real crowd pleaser. It was based on a personal theory of his. Namely: "If a ham is precooked (and it usually says so right on the label) then there's no reason why you can't put it on the old barbecue." He also topped off his ham fillets with pineapple slices that had been soaked in enough rum to make a pirate silly. No real problem with Helen or Jack.

Cindy and Roy promised to be in charge of entertainment. They would bring along their croquet set, their badminton set, and Nerf balls for the kids. Herbert's brother Don, a higher-up at the Good Humor company, had promised to furnish dessert. "Enough Creamsicles to make everyone sick," he said with that well-known laugh in his voice.

Peggy's eyelids began to relax and actually shut for a moment or two as she thought about her husband's role in the festivities. She knew that she could always count on Herb. Herb's duties were to supervise the parking and run the after-dinner slide show. By Herb's calculation, there were seven hundred and twenty-six slides in all. He took an entire day off from work to organize them in chronological order. They began with the very early "Zanesville Years," progressed through the "North Zanesville Years," the "Berea years," the "Two Months in Tulsa," all of his own slides from Germany, right up to last year's get-together.

Herb was sound asleep. You could always tell when Herb was really sound asleep. He made a sort of purring sound. It wasn't a snore and it wasn't a wheeze, it was really purring. He was dreaming about seats for a Chicago Bears game, but there was this half-girl, half-lizard that needed them more than he did. That's all he would remember.

Peggy's mother and father were equally sound asleep on the rented double bed in the guestroom. They had been houseguests for the past eleven days, and as far as they knew, tomorrow would be just like the last two Sundays. A little more breakfast than usual, a chance to read the paper, take a little nap, a casserole of some sort for dinner, watch *60 Minutes*, and go to bed.

Peggy was still wide awake, a condition she described as "my brain won't shut up." Doilies, she thought. Her mother always loved doilies. Why hadn't she gotten doilies for all of the furniture? Maybe she should try and borrow some first thing tomorrow from someone in her church group. Bad idea. Mother would see her putting them around and know that something was up. Peggy reconciled herself to a doilyless party and went on to the next order of business on her brain list: what to do about the garbage. She had purchased seven boxes of the new twist-top Hefty bags and was sure they would do the job. The problem was where to put them. Not too near the food but not too far away either, since the kids would all be using paper plates and kids tend to dribble if they have to carry anything too far. Maybe next to the shed. No, the kids would trample the new marigolds. Maybe not, though. Not if the can was a few feet away from the marigolds. Herb could spray-paint one of the garbage cans early in the morning, and if it dried as fast as the Krylon people said it would, she would have time to put some decals on it so it wouldn't look like a garbage can and people might still want to sit there.

She tried to recall what decals she had left in her decal drawer as the rain picked up momentum. It sounded like thousands of mice dancing on the aluminum awnings. Herb stopped purring for a moment, shifted his weight so that most of the covers went his way, and resumed purring.

I'll just have Herb keep an eye on the can, Peggy thought. When it gets looking full he can take it down to the garage and put in a new Hefty bag.

The rain began to beat like bullets, and Peggy realized that if she was going to get any sleep at all she would have to organize the rest of her thoughts like a shopping list. She conjured up a small piece of brain paper and found a little brain pencil. It was either that or go to the kitchen and do it for real, and that would keep her up all night. Her mental list began as follows:

1. Wake up before anyone else does.
2. Pour the cream in the fruit salad.
3. Put it in the freezer.

4. Call Uncle Buddy and remind him not to forget his camera.
5. See if the lawn needs another sweeping.
6. Sweep it if it does.
7. Put on nail polish.
8. Make sure Herb is up in time to spray-paint the garbage can.
9. Call Buddy again and tell him to bring his flash attachment in case the rain keeps up.

These were the top nine, but there were thousands of other thoughts racing through her mind. Things like, Where did I put that little Japanese book that shows you how to make radishes into roses? and, My God, I never even counted Herb and myself, so that would make twenty-two!

The rain continued to increase to the point it could no longer just be rain. It turned into hail. At first the hailstones were simply harmless little opalescent M & M's, but soon they matured into the size of runt tangerines. The sound of the ice balls on the aluminum awnings was such that even Herb woke up. "Take the goddamn tickets, Mrs. Lizard," he said, sitting bolt upright in their bed. Herb always dovetailed his dreams into his real life.

The hail continued until five in the morning. Peggy left her bed, wondering how her parents could sleep through such a cacophony, and re-Windexed the tables and countertops. Herb was also unable to get back to sleep, and decided to spray-paint the garbage can right then and there.

By six-thirty most of the hailstones had melted in the warmth of the rising new day, but a mist still hung in the air. It was the kind of mist that young white lovers think of as "England." It was the kind of mist that Peggy and Herb thought of as "How in the hell are we gonna rearrange the furniture and set up card tables or whatever so that we can get twenty-two people into this house?"

The mist took its cue from a loud thunderclap and reverted back into a slow drizzle. It was obvious that the usually reliable Orange County sun had decided to take the day off. Around five of seven or so Herb and Peggy sat down at the kitchen table, each with a cup of Nescafé, and devised Plan B. Plan B consisted of the following maneuvers. First, Herb went down to the basement and brought up four Bekins moving boxes, each about two feet square and roughly the same in height. Two went in the living room between the couches and two went in the entryway.

Peggy went to the linen closet, selected four of her more brightly colored print sheets, and wrapped each of the boxes.

The thought behind it was this: four people at each box. That made sixteen. Four people at the table—that made twenty—and she and Herb could eat off the coffee table like they usually did. That made twenty-two. Peggy took all of her non-essential decorator cushions and made little stacks of them at each of the corners of the moving boxes. She had just enough pillows for eighteen little "seats." As for the other two moving-box seats, Herb used a whole roll of Bounty cleaning off two of the lawn chairs. It didn't really match, but at this point that was no longer an issue. Peggy, in her desperation, had long since given up the idea of elegance. In fact it didn't even phase her, as it normally would, when Herb looked at the Bekins Boxes shrouded in their Peter Max prints and said, "Christ, it looks like we're having a fag dog show here!"

Then, as is so often the case, things began to happen all at once. The rain kicked itself into second gear; Peggy put a Swingline staple in the heel of her hand as she attempted to affix the Kleenex flowers to the doorway; Herb, who had decided to take his shower, got shampoo in his eye and ran, dripping and naked, into the kitchen to pour some bottled water into the affected orb; and Jack and Helen arrived with a cooler full of garni.

When the doorbell rang Peggy was busy putting several Band-Aids over her puncture so that she wouldn't drip any blood into the fruit salad. Fearing that the doorbell's insistence might wake up his in-laws, Herb quickly put on one of Peggy's little party aprons and, one hand on his shampooed eye, the other on his exposed backside, he dashed to the door and opened it.

Helen let out a little scream and immediately put her purse in front of her face to black out the terrible vision.

Peggy emerged from the bathroom, still holding the can of Band-Aids, and let out a slightly louder scream than Helen's. Herb turned and dashed into the bathroom. "You better take over, honey," he said to his wife.

Jack began laughing so hard that he dropped the cheap Styrofoam K-Mart cooler and it cracked wide open, spilling carrot strips, celery stalks filled with peanut butter, and olives all over the porch steps. The five dozen olives rolled all the way to the front gate just as it opened, announcing the arrival of Uncle Buddy.

"Jesus Christ," he bellowed. "Your hail is green!"

Jack started laughing again, this time so hard that he patted his jacket pocket to make sure he had remembered his heart pills. Helen fell to her knees and started gathering what undamaged garni there was.

"Sweetheart, just leave that," Peggy said nicely. "We'll just go with the nut cups, and you're getting soaked." Peggy ushered everyone into the entryway.

Buddy set the two thoroughly soaked cases of Almaden Mountain White Chablis on one of the little Bekins tables, and it collapsed instantly. Herb emerged at this point in a much more modest bathrobe. He told Peggy not to worry. "Me and Jack and Buddy will rig up something for a table." The three men headed for the basement.

Halfway down the walk, the three men ran smack-dab into Frances, and Herb's brother Don. "Cheese balls," chirped Frances, holding up a large white Tupperware wastebasket. "And two tons of Creamsicles in my trunk if one of you bozos could give me a hand," added Don. Frances and Don continued on into the rain-soaked entryway. Frances set her cheese-ball basket on the other little Bekins table and it collapsed immediately. "Don't worry about it," Peggy said, smiling. "Herb and the boys have got the situation under control."

At that moment Cindy and Roy and their children Stacey and Tracy drove up honking their horn like they always did. They popped out of their station wagon, each identically attired in a yellow raincoat and rain hat with yellow boots to match.

Roy, as you may recall, was the "entertainment chairman" for the event. He had his arms full of boxed games in honor of the rainy day. Chutes And Ladders, Candy Land, and Chinese checkers for the kids; Boggle and Life for the grown-ups. Cindy, though not asked, had taken it upon herself to make an enormous fruit salad. Peggy welcomed them at the door with towels. "God," said Cindy, pointing to the well-mashed garni on the front steps, "did Uncle Buddy get sick already?"

The three "table experts" dripped back into the house, empty-handed. "It's not a dead issue yet," said Herb. "I'm still thinking what we might have." Peggy ushered them into the kitchen with the others. In a matter of a split second, everyone had a fresh cup of Nescafé and the kids had Ovaltine. Peggy did a body count. "There's eleven of us so far. That's enough for a surprise. Let's wake up Mom and Dad."

The adults all had one last bracing belt of Nescafé and followed the tiptoeing children through the laundry area to the door of the guest-room. Peggy would give a count of three, Herb would push the door open, and everyone would holler, "Surprise!" That was the plan.

Peggy positioned herself right in front of the door with Herb next to her, his hand firmly on the knob. The others hunkered quietly behind them. "One," said Peggy. Herb tightened his grip.

"Two," whispered Stacey and Tracy.

"Three!" shouted everyone.

And then there was a deafening "Surprise!" as Herb turned the door knob and pushed.

The door would not open.

There was nothing wrong with the knob; it turned just fine. The problem had to do with the rain, the chilling effect of the hail, and the automatic response of the central heating system. The door had swollen shut. Herb put his weight into it. Nothing. Jack and Herb put their combined weight into it. Nothing. Nothing except for the fact that all of the shouting and banging had thoroughly awakened Peggy's parents. They had been aware of the swollen-door problem for several hours and had finally fallen asleep after a night of pounding and screaming that had been drowned out by the tap dance of the hailstones on the aluminum awnings.

"Peggy, this isn't funny," her mother said. "Your father had to go this morning and couldn't get out of the bedroom."

"We're doing everything we can," said Herb.

Peggy's mother was almost yelling by now. "We *both* had to go. *I* held *mine!* Your father ended up having to use the blue vase with the dried flowers."

"They're not that dry anymore," laughed her father, quickly adding, "I'll get you a new vase, Pumpkin."

Peggy's mother put in the final nail. "I didn't spend fifty years with your father just to watch him piss in a flowerpot. Now, I don't know who in the hell is out there with you, but somebody better figure out how to open this goddamn door!"

The group split into factions. Jack, Buddy, and Don went to Don's car to get the crowbar that Don thought might be somewhere under the Creamsicles.

The girls made more Nescafé and, braving the elements, removed a screen from the guestroom window and passed the cups into Mom and Dad. Mom cautioned her husband. "Howard, you know what coffee does to you. If I were you I wouldn't."

Herb started scouring the neighborhood for a chain saw.

It was the chain saw that finally did the trick. There was a roar of noise when it finally started up, accompanied by billowing clouds of black smoke and gasoline fumes. "Stand back," Herb ordered.

In a little over twenty minutes Herb was able to cut out the center panel of the door. It fell with a slap onto the laundry-room floor. It was like a Clint Eastwood "escape" movie. As the smoke and dust began to clear, Mom and Dad could be seen heading through the opening to freedom. Herb felt like Rambo. "All clear, and everyone's fine," he shouted triumphantly.

Mom sprinted for the master bath. Tracy was in there. "I'll be out in a sec," she said. Mom made a beeline for the other bathroom. Stacey was in there. "Give me a minute," she said. Mom turned the color of a fresh plum, and her husband jokingly offered the vase.

By eleven-thirty that night all of the guests had left and Herb once again was purring. Peggy crawled in next to him. All in all, I think everyone had a pretty good time, she thought to herself. Dear, sweet Herb made a dandy little table out of the sawn-out door. The kids didn't break anything and they loved the Creamsicles. The cheese balls were a hit and so was the fruit salad. Dad told his Jewish joke and everyone laughed. Buddy never got sick, even with all that gasoline smell, and there were only twenty-two slides left to go when the projector bulb burned out.

Peggy drifted off to sleep. Now her only worry was what all that rain might have done to her marigolds.

8

On the Couch

Jerry Butts, forty-three, had a problem. Since the age of sixteen, he had been plagued by a persistent nightmare that he couldn't shake. It was always the same: he is walking down the produce aisle at his local Safeway, stark naked. He knows people are laughing, but he doesn't know why. He keeps shopping as if nothing's wrong. A long-legged high school girl in gym shorts stops and asks about strawberries, but he's too tongue-tied to answer, so he snickers and leaves. He finally decides to make a mad rush for the parking lot, leaving his groceries behind, when suddenly a very fat woman blocks his way through the turnstile. She grabs him and starts to kiss and fondle him passionately. He's getting very aroused. People start gathering around, pointing at his privates and taking pictures. He's now stuck between the fat lady and the throng of shoppers. He starts to howl like a sick dog. Suddenly the fat lady turns into a chicken. He grabs her by the legs and runs out the door. The Safeway goes up in a fiery blaze, and Jerry wakes up in a cold sweat.

Jerry decided to seek professional help.

DOCTOR: Do you spell that with one or two Ts, Mr. Butts?

JERRY: One, I mean *two*, Dr. Steele, but what does that have to do with my dream?

DOCTOR: Just getting my records straight, Jerry, no cause for alarm.

JERRY: You know, I don't believe in this head-shrinking malarkey, Doc. I want you to know that right up front. I never have and I never will. It's too fuzzy around the edges. So don't try to provoke me and get me to say something sick about my mother, because I won't buy it. I don't know why I'm here, really. I just figured that after twenty-seven years of the same dream I should find some way to flush it out of my system, you know what I mean? I sure could never bring it up with my wife. She'd think it was about her weight problem.

DOCTOR: Your wife has a weight problem?

JERRY: No, she's just fat, I'm the one with the problem! [laughing] Just kidding. Listen, she's a wonderful mother and a great cook, and I wouldn't trade her for the world. Hey, I'm no prize, either. Let's just leave her out of this, okay?

DOCTOR: Sure, Jerry, if it's too painful to talk about . . .

JERRY: There you go again, putting words into my mouth. I didn't say anything about "painful"! Cecilia wasn't even around when I first had this godawful dream and anyway, she's no heave-o like the chicken-lady in the checkout line. You're grasping at straws, Doc, you're pitching horseshoes in the dark . . .

DOCTOR: Jerry, psychoanalysis is an inexact science . . .

JERRY: You're telling me.

DOCTOR: Jerry, why are you sweating?

JERRY: Because I know what you're going to ask next.

DOCTOR: What do you suspect?

JERRY: Oh, something like . . . [mimicking Doctor] "Jerry, do you find your wife repulsive? Jerry, how often do you masturbate? Jerry, did your mother ever catch you? Did you like it?"

DOCTOR: Is that what you want to talk about, Jerry?

JERRY: Not on your life! That's none of your business. Your business is this cockamamy dream. Just work a little of your mumbo jumbo on that pesky heap of dung so I can get out of here in one piece!

DOCTOR: Okay, fine. Jerry, let's talk about chickens. Are you a pet lover? I mean,

in the traditional sense? Have you ever
owned a pet?

JERRY: Yes.

DOCTOR: A chicken?

JERRY: A dog.

DOCTOR: I see.

JERRY: You can't keep a chicken in the city.

DOCTOR: But you'd like to if you could. Is that
what you're telling me?

JERRY: There you go again. I'm telling you I
have a dog. That's all. Does that make
me a psycho?

DOCTOR: Of course it doesn't. What's the dog's
name?

JERRY: I call her Chicken.

DOCTOR: I'm gonna write this down, Jerry. It
might be a problem. Tell me your feel-
ings about Chicken.

JERRY: [agitated] Now, that really ticks me
off! To come here and pay you a hundred and fifty dollars and have you sit
there and accuse me of having un-
natural thoughts about my dog, now
that's the last straw . . .

DOCTOR: Jerry, please, calm down, you misunderstood . . .

JERRY: The hell I misunderstood! You've been
driving at this the whole time. First
you make fun of my name, like everyone in high school did *every day*, then
you pick on my wife for a while, making her out to be a worthless sack of

potatoes, then you start in on my love
of dogs. Next you'll probably go after
the fact that I've never been in a
fistfight and that once in Chicago a
man pinched my wife on the butt and I
just walked real fast the other way and
that I'm stuck in a boring job at the
post office and take orders from a black
woman and will never be my own boss
and see myself as a wimp and a jerk
that will never get to Europe, never be
able to afford a big-screen TV, and will
always cut a wide berth around the
produce section of any major super-
market. That's it, isn't it? That's how
you have me pegged. Well, I'll tell you
something, Herr Doctor, I may not be a
superman like Sylvester Stallone or
George Bush, but I'm no Charlie Man-
son, either. I can live without big-
screen TV and fresh produce, and
there's nothing wrong with me that a
little talking-to-the-mirror can't handle, so get off my case, okay?

DOCTOR: Mr. Butts, I think you're right. I think
you just cured yourself. Sure, we could
dance around that butt-pinching incident for a while, but if that's as scary
as it gets, you're not headed for the
funny farm, I assure you. Next time
you see that fat lady in the dream, give
her a big hug back. Maybe the chicken

will run away and you can finish your shopping.

JERRY: That's it? One session and I'm cured? I thought I'd be sitting here moaning and groaning for the rest of my life! A guy down at the office, Butch Jenkins, got drunk one night and told me he'd been seeing a shrink for nine fuckin' years and still can't get over the habit of sending naked pictures of his wife to *Hustler* magazine. Boy, he ought to come see you.

DOCTOR: Good idea. Be sure he brings the pictures.

JERRY: No problem. I've seen 'em, they're good. Listen, to change the subject, I *do* find my wife repulsive and . . .

DOCTOR: Sorry, time's up. Read my book.

9
Canterbury Tale

Any reputable real-estate person will tell you that it doesn't make good sense to have the nicest house on the block. Pat and Patty Patterson never dreamed that would be a problem for them when they moved into 3301 Canterbury. Their one-story two-bedroom one-bath bungalow was smaller than the adjacent house by a third and the misty dotted-Swiss curtains did little to perk up the gun-metal gray of the aging house paint. They kept their windows washed and their lawn mowed, but then who didn't? For twenty years every Saturday morning was concert time for the Canterbury Street lawn-mower symphony.

Then the neighborhood blew open like the bottom of a wet bag of garbage. The Henleys retired and moved to Florida. The Crenshaws decided to live full-time on their boat. Bill Phillips finally perfected his collapsible Christmas-tree stand and took the whole business to Dearborn where he could be near his daughter. And so on, and so on. Soon all but three houses on Canterbury were on the market. "It'll be interesting to see what they go for," mused Pat.

They didn't go for much. The street became a "buyer's market." The Henleys' house, a scant eight feet away from the Pattersons', went to a Yugoslavian travel agent named Blatski and his wife. The husband, a bit hard of hearing, spent most of every day listening to Berlitz English records at top volume. His wife, an affable, rotund woman who spoke very little of any language, immediately dug up the Henleys' lawn and planted potatoes.

Soon the house on the other side of the Pattersons' was sold as well. The new owners were two pencil-thin men who dry-cleaned their designer jeans. Their first act as homeowners was to put reflective Mylar in the windows and bar them up. They kept strange hours and it seemed like most of their friends had limousines. If it wasn't for the uniquely human problem of a runny nose, they could have been easily mistaken for a couple of very tall, very thin owls.

Next the house across the street was boosted onto blocks and escorted down the street on a flatbed truck. All that was left was a hole in the ground that contained an old water heater and a Ping-Pong table with no net. Soon, by default, the Pattersons had the nicest house on the block. That's when they started house hunting.

———

Generally, they would just put Freckles in the back of the station wagon, opening the rear window a crack so she wouldn't throw up, and head off, aimlessly looking for the familiar red pennants that announced that it was perfectly permissible to come inside and poke around in a complete stranger's closets.

On Sundays, however, it was "get down to business." Pat and Patty would pour themselves a second cup of Sanka and hunker over the real-estate section of the paper. Pat would make ball-point-pen circles around anything that seemed like a possibility.

In order to qualify as a possibility, a house had to live up to the following checklist.

1. It had to be in the tricounty area.
2. It had to sound too good to be true.
3. It couldn't be the nicest house on the block.

Pat would take the real-estate section and fold it in thirds, and then fold it in thirds again so it would fit into his jacket pocket. Patty would make two peanut-butter sandwiches and put them in Ziploc bags, and off they'd go.

On this particular Sunday it was gray and drizzling. The Pattersons actually preferred that. They figured if a place looked good in bad weather, it could only look better when the sun came out.

The first house they saw was way too big for them. They liked all of the built-ins, but it was just too darn big. The second house might have been a real consideration, but it had sold itself a half hour earlier.

The third house on the list was the one with two red circles around it. It had gotten an A plus on the checklist and was close enough to their current home so that Patty wouldn't have to change her shopping habits.

Here's what the ad had said:

SLICE OF HEAVEN!

2 plus 3 plus 1½, yr. rnd. tulip gdn. Full cable t.v. serv. Must see.

Pat and Patty weren't sure that they had the right address. When they pulled up all they saw was an elderly couple sitting on aluminum lawn chairs in a yard full of tulips. No pennants, no "for sale" sign, no nothing.

Patty hit her power window and called out to the couple. "Is this the open house?" she asked.

"Yep, sure is," the man responded. "That's why we're sitting out front. Usually we sit out back."

The man's name was Archie Cavanaugh and his wife's name was Glenda. Archie had retired three years ago after forty-one years as a milkman—the "cow-juice business," as he liked to call it.

The Cavanaughs met the Pattersons at the small picket-fence gate. Archie unlatched it and turned to Pat. "I'm gonna let you open it so you can see how smooth it swings. I used to have it opening in instead of out, but it made a creaky noise so I switched it around. Go ahead, open her up. Shut it behind you and come on in."

Pat opened the gate and ushered his wife up the two short steps. Then he entered as well and shut the gate behind him.

"Well?" said Mr. Cavanaugh.

"Well, what?" said Pat Patterson.

"Did you hear any creaking?" said Mr. Cavanaugh.

"I don't think so," said Pat Patterson.

"What'd I tell you," said Mr. Cavanaugh.

The quartet reached the front stoop of the house, and Glenda put a tentative hand on Patty's shoulder.

"Did you notice the tulips?" she asked.

"They're absolutely beautiful," said Patty, smiling.

Glenda winked. "Fish emulsion," she said. "The smell goes away in about four days, and the tulips go bananas."

"I'll remember that," said Patty with sincere interest.

The inside of the house was a museum of white ingenuity. Mr. Cavanaugh was probably a good milkman, but after a cursory tour of the house it became apparent that he was a stellar handyman.

With all due respect to the art of architecture, no home is ever perfect. After forty-one years in the same dwelling, the Cavanaughs had been faced with their share of problems, and Archie pointed with pride to his solutions.

"Look at this," he said, opening the pantry closet door. Instantly an ironing board shot into the room like a bayonet. Then he opened the pantry door a little wider; there was a barely audible click, and thanks to an elaborate set of ropes and pulleys the ironing board retracted and shot straight up into the attic. "There when you need it, gone when you don't," said Archie. They walked into the living room. Archie put his hand on a wall switch and said, "Hold on to your hats."

With one flick of the switch he achieved the following: the drapes closed themselves, the lights dimmed, and the TV went on. "That one was a ball-buster to wire up," he whispered to Pat.

There were trap-door garbage chutes, self-loading toilet-paper dispensers, and two ceiling-mounted pot-and-pan holders that spun.

The foursome moved into the breakfast nook. Glenda had insisted that they have coffee and, after they learned that it was Sanka, the Pattersons accepted. The house felt good. Warm and good. Patty was thinking about what Freckles might do to the tulips if they lived here. Pat was thinking about escrow. "What kind of offers have you been getting?" Pat asked of the Cavanaughs.

There was a silence that felt like the freeze-frame at the end of a bad mystery movie.

Glenda broke the silence with a little giggle.

"Well, we've got our coffee," she said. "Now how about something to go with it? We've got dough-nuts, Danish, and toast."

Patty opened her purse and took out the Ziploc bag containing the peanut-butter sandwiches. "That's very sweet of you, Mrs. Cavanaugh," she said, "but we've got these and it's only ten-thirty."

"Brunch!" squealed Glenda.

"Let me get them some plates for those," said Archie. "We don't want to see good friends eating off the bare table." Archie quickly grabbed two commemorative plates off of a display shelf in the nook. One commemorated Truman, the other the discovery of radium.

Patty placed their peanut-butter sandwiches on the commemorative plates.

"So," Pat said, trying his best to get back to business, "is the place listed with anyone, or are you trying to sell it yourself?"

"Sell it?" said Mrs. Cavanaugh.

"Why on earth would I want to sell it?" asked Mr. Cavanaugh.

Patty had one of those flashes of female intui-tion that told her, You're in a house with luna-tics. She quickly picked up the uneaten parts of the peanut-butter sandwiches and put them back into the Ziploc bag.

"Well," she said, "we have about a hundred places to go today, and we don't want to take up your time."

Pat was a little slower in the intuition department. He asked a serious question. "This place *is* for sale, isn't it?"

Archie laughed like Walter Brennan. "Where would we go?"

"I don't understand," said Pat.

"Not that many people do," said Glenda with a smile that is acceptable only in sanitariums and Georgia. She took a belt of Sanka. "Let me tell you a little bit about us Cavanaughs," she said. "We're not sticks-in-the-mud like Archie's brother and . . . what's her name?"

"His wife? I forget," said Archie.

"Exactly," said Glenda. "We *like* people."

Archie finally took off his baseball cap. "But we don't meet that many," he said. "That's why we do these open houses. Last week we had a guy in here all the way from Piedmont."

"Didn't he have a friend that knew your sister?" asked Glenda.

"I can't really remember, honey. You might be right, but I can't really remember," said Archie.

Patty seized the moment. She rose in a semidefiant attitude, indicating: "Time's up." "Well, *we're* certainly going to keep in touch, aren't we, Pat?"

Pat read the tone in his wife's voice correctly and started ushering her to the front door. "Oh, you betcha," he said. "We don't meet people like you folks every day."

Archie opened the door for them. "Would you like to see the ironing board again?" he said.

"We've really got to be running along, Archie," said Pat.

Glenda wedged herself in the doorway, blocking any possibility of leaving. "Listen," she said. "You folks wouldn't happen to be *Falcon Crest* fans, would you?"

"Not really," answered Patty.

"Oh," said Glenda. "I was just thinking that if you *were*, then Fridays would be a great time for us all to get together."

Archie Cavanaugh put a "that's enough" hand on his wife's shoulder. "These are busy people," he said. "We'll see them whenever *they* have the chance."

Glenda gave way and they all proceeded to the small picket-fence gate.

Archie opened it. This time Pat could swear he heard a little creaking—not enough to wake the neighborhood, but enough to drive you a little bit nuts if you listened for things like that.

———

The Pattersons saw only two more houses that day. The first was crawling with Cambodians and virtually impossible to see. The second had more mirrors than a fun house and made Patty dizzy. Freckles was getting antsy anyway, so they went home.

They pulled into the driveway and Freckles bounded out of the car, over the fence, and ate one of the Blatskis' potatoes. Then he bounded back, happy to be home.

So were Pat and Patty.

Pat and Patty had not spoken to each other that

much during the day. In fact, they didn't say a word on the way home, but their thoughts were in sync.

Pat entered the house, poured himself a beer, and silently took his wife's hand. Then he led her to the front stoop, where they sat down. "You know something, Patty," he said. "There's nothing wrong with having the best house on the block. That's what kings had. That's what the president has. That's what Dan Rather probably has. And that's what *we* have."

Patty reached for his beer mug. "Can I have a sip?" she said.

"You can have your own if you want," said Pat. "We've got plenty."

10

Second Best

Jack Perkins loved his office. He especially loved it on Sunday afternoons when no one was around. It was more like church than church itself. It was a rare Sunday that he didn't excuse himself after lunch and head for the office to "catch up on the backlog." His wife Diane didn't seem to mind. She was always up to something, like between-meal snacking. His son, Little Jack, hated Sundays and was never around himself.

Jack was a lawyer, specializing in real estate, and always had plenty of backlog. By the time he finished with the current stack of escrow contracts, his beloved Sunday at the office was almost over. Still, he had an hour or so to kill before Diane would call about dinner. This was "golden time." He considered his options. He could sip Jack Daniels and watch *Lee Trevino's Golf Tips* on video, always a boon to his game. Or he could delve into his investment portfolio and move some of his money around, the closest thing to an endless round of Monopoly in a grown man's life. Or he could just stretch out on the

Naugahyde couch, stare at all the mementos and commendations that lined his office walls, and let his mind drift back to that crack in time he liked to call "Jack Perkins—the Early Years."

Today, like most days, he homed in on Oakland, California, June 1962. There was Jackie Kennedy on TV, waving to the camera. *Camelot* was in full swing and young Jack Perkins felt like Sir Lancelot. He had just gotten out of the Army, was 1600 miles from home, and had time to kill. They wouldn't expect him home until he called, and he wasn't about to do that yet. For once in his life he wanted to cut loose, and he knew just who to call. Toby Tyler. Toby the Tease.

Toby was a girl from high school who now lived in San Francisco. Jack had always admired her from afar, her aloof manner, her caked-on makeup and lacquered auburn hair, her matching angora skirt-and-sweater sets. She had grace, beauty, charm, all the things that made her a friendless outcast among her classmates. Most dismissed her as a stuck-up bitch, but Jack knew otherwise. He knew she was his ticket to supreme sexual bliss. Unfortunately, he never acted on his conviction, and she left town immediately after graduation and never looked back. Now he could make his move.

He was shaking like a leaf when he first phoned her from the lobby of the San Francisco YMCA. It took her a few minutes to place him, but once she did he quickly recovered and asked her out for a drink. She didn't hesitate to say yes and named the time and place. Jack knew that all those years of unacknowledged compliments about her hair and unrequited invites to the Youth Canteen would finally pay off. Toby the Tease was his!

She didn't show. He stood around this creepy bar full of Italians and beatniks for four hours, fending off gibes about wandering away from the Gray Line Tour, and then retired to the Y. He had been *had*, like thousands of guys before him, by the Tease. She was probably sitting around right now with some of her snooty San Francisco friends having a good laugh about this hometown bumpkin she had just snookered. He felt like he deserved it.

He didn't know what to do. Toby was his one idea for cutting loose. He went to the filthiest porno movie he could find, but that didn't help. He liked the movie, but was still depressed. He thought of calling her again and got drunk enough one night to do it. She wasn't there.

He finally wired home that he was back onshore and gave his mom the train schedule. She was thrilled and that made him feel a little better. He packed up and headed for the San Francisco train station. He was ready to get out of that burg.

He remembered dozing off at the train station. He could feel someone shaking his arm, and as he awoke there was Toby, like a dreamy Grace Kelly, smiling into his eyes. She was so beautiful. He reached out and touched her lacquered hair to assure himself she was really there.

She had just leaned over to give him a kiss when the office phone rang and destroyed Jack's stroll down memory lane. It was Diane. Dinner was getting cold and *60 Minutes* had already started. Was he still a part of this family?

After four servings of cold creamed chipped beef on toast, Jack stayed up late reading a new book on *Hitler in Hollywood*, a little-known period in Der Führer's life before his rise to power. His mind drifted and he couldn't stop comparing Toby and Diane. Toby tended to come out ahead in all categories. As he watched Diane sleeping soundly, he began to wonder. Who is this woman? What do I really know about her? What does she do all day? Does she have some secret life I know nothing about? After thinking about it for a few minutes, he decided she didn't and fell asleep.

But the thought wouldn't go away. Jack had long ago learned to trust his gut, and his gut told him that something was amiss in his marriage, something insidious, something that was changing Diane from a loving wife into a total stranger. He turned to his best friend, Tom Pendleton, for advice.

"Jack, if you want my opinion, you're just bored with the woman, that's all. Take a trip to Vegas, check into Caesar's Palace, and call up Morty's Escort Service. That'll clean out your pipes."

Vegas didn't help. By the time Jack returned Diane was more withdrawn and uncommunicative than ever. He'd come home early from the office and she'd be sitting in the den, watching reruns of *The Newlywed Game* and crying. He tried to interest her in going out to a movie or dinner, and she always had something else planned, like catching up on family birthday cards or doing the crossword puzzle in *TV Guide*. The more he poked and prodded into her private world, the more she seemed to resent it. He retreated to his office and distant memories of Toby the Tease.

After Toby found him in the train station that fateful day, Jack's life took a left turn. He took Toby to a fancy pizzeria that night, and she poured her heart out. She loved San Francisco, but was alone and scared. She had no friends, no job, no money. When Jack called, she was afraid he would laugh at her misfortune. Then she realized how much he could help. Would he help her?

Jack ended up staying in San Francisco all summer. He spent his entire Army savings helping Toby create a new life for herself, a life he felt privileged to share. Every night before returning to his place at the Y, they would sit on the floor in Toby's new apartment on Nob Hill, drinking red wine, listening to Dave Brubeck on her new stereo, and reading e.e. cummings. Every night he would profess his love for her, and Toby would give him a peck on the cheek and tell him what a sweet boy he was. He knew she meant it with all her heart and that it was only a matter of time before she invited him into her bedroom.

That never happened. Toby found a great job in advertising, and Jack ran out of money by summer's end and had to return home to his mom and his future. Sitting at the same spot in the train station as before, Jack asked Toby to marry him. She said she had to think about it. It would mean leaving her new job and moving back to the Midwest while Jack went to college and law school. It would mean returning to a place where everyone thought she was a stuck-up bitch. It would mean sacrifice and hardship and monogamy. Jack left town without an answer.

Again, the phone jangled in his office and broke his reverie. It was Little Jack. "Dad, you better come home. I think that Mom is flipping out."

This time it was serious. When Jack got home Diane was in the upstairs bedroom with the door locked, crying. The story from Little Jack was this: over dinner Little Jack had said something thoughtless about experimenting with Diane's stuffed green peppers as coyote bait, and she blew her top. She demanded that he leave the table immediately and vacuum the whole house. Little Jack tried to apologize, but she was not to be reasoned with. As he ran the vacuum, she stood over him, pointing out dust kitties and gnashing her teeth. Then she retired to the bathroom.

As a way of bringing peace to the household, Jack let the matter ride, but he stayed up all that night trying to get at the root cause of Diane's problem. By dawn he had boiled it down to two possibilities: a complete nervous breakdown, or drugs. His gut said drugs. It sounded farfetched, but how else could he explain the shell she had built around herself? According to the papers, it happens all the time in the best of families, which this surely was. Diane was the least likely person to suspect, he thought. All the more reason to suspect her.

He needed evidence. First thing the next morning, before anyone else was up, he began his search. He didn't hesitate to rifle through her most personal effects, digging for that empty pill bottle or errant coke spoon that he might use to wrench a confession out of her. Unfortunately, she covered her tracks well. He found nothing that screamed "dope addict."

All he had to go on was her behavior, he decided, which was increasingly bizarre. That's what he got from the stack of books on how to spot drug problems at home that he checked out of the library. "Garbage in, garbage out," one said. "Where there's smoke, there's fire," said another. "What you don't know *can* hurt you," said a third, "and you are probably being hurt as you read this." Jack was starting to get steamed. He saw Diane's drug problem as a personal affront.

How dare she, he thought as he settled into another Sunday at the office. Where does she get off betraying me and Little Jack like that?

How come I married her in the first place?

She was his little sister's best friend, and he had known her since they were kids. He had even taken her out a couple of times in high school, but only as a "good friend." That she was, especially after that summer in San Francisco. Every day he went to her house and cried his eyes out about Toby the Tease, never mentioning her by name, of course. Diane thought he was suffering from combat fatigue and insisted on nursing him back to health. What could he do? She didn't look like Grace Kelly, but she was there, she had always been there, and she would always be there. Until now, that is. Now she was slipping away.

"Oh, why, Toby, why?" he cried out, distraught. "Why didn't you love me like I loved you! It's all your fault! If you hadn't abandoned me, then I wouldn't have married Diane, and if I hadn't married Diane, she wouldn't have become a drug addict, and if she hadn't become a drug addict, my life wouldn't be ruined!" In Jack's mind, the cards were stacked against him.

He decided that he should warn Little Jack about his mother before it was too late. He rushed home and knocked on the door of his bedroom, but the boy wasn't there. He tiptoed past Diane's bedroom; he didn't want to set off another drug-crazed tantrum. He looked everywhere in the house, but no Little Jack.

Before calling the police, he decided to check one more place. Behind the garage. Sure enough, there he was, sucking on a marijuana cigarette when Jack snuck up on him. Little Jack started to run, but Jack tackled him and pinned him to the ground. Little Jack was terrified. He was sure that his dad was going to kill him. He had Son of Sam written all over his face.

Jack had his hands around the boy's neck, shouting, "Where did you get this stuff, you little ingrate? Who's turned you into a shiftless, good-for-nothing, headed-for-the-big-house drug addict? Your mother?"

Little Jack was paralyzed with fear. "Yes," he peeped.

"Just as I figured," Jack said. He released his son's neck and headed toward the house. Now the moment had finally arrived. The moment he could finally confront his wife for betraying him with her disgusting weakness and even turning his only begotten son against him. He couldn't wait.

Diane was quietly reading the Hitler book in bed when he burst into the room. "Diane," he shouted, "your drug days are up! And after all I've done for you, after all the years I've stood by you and given you this lovely home and food for your table and clothes for your back and—"

Diane cut him off. "Oh, shut up, Jack Perkins, just shut up!" She threw the book at his head, but missed. "I don't know what you're talking about and neither do you. But don't tell me what *you've* given *me*. You concocted a happy home for yourself to drop by once in a while, and I just happen to be another piece of furniture, a piece of furniture that cooks and plays Scramble. You've never really loved me. You're still in love with

Toby the Tease! You didn't think I knew, did you? You didn't think I was smart enough to know. Well, Jack, you shouldn't talk in your sleep . . .

Jack was stunned. In that one brief instant it all became clear. He had been living a lie and Diane had just told him the truth.

And he spent the rest of his life making it up to her.

11

The Color Beige

The first year at Bromfield Musical Tech was the same for everybody: basic sight-reading, notation, theory, and English. It wasn't until the second year that Buzzy could devote his entire time to the clarinet. Likewise, it wasn't until that second September that Rayfield, or "Slats," as he liked to be called, could concentrate full-time on his tenor sax.

Buzzy Albright had a dream of becoming the next Pete Fountain. Slats Williams had a dream of becoming the next John Coltrane. Neither one ever dreamed that economics would force them into the position of roommates. But here they were, and here they would stay for the next three years.

The first two months were the toughest for Buzzy. He would spend his nights locked in the bathroom trying to perfect the opening bars of "Stranger on the Shore" while Slats and his black brothers had a jam session on "Salt Peanuts" in the other room. One night Buzzy asked if he could sit in. He did his best, but it was mere moments before the group decided to stop playing.

Slats and Buzzy stayed up late that night. Slats did most of the talking. It was the beginning of an education that Buzzy would never forget.

Buzzy was a fast learner. It was only a matter of weeks before he had grown what he thought was a goatee, started tapping his foot on subway trains, and referred to everyone as "man."

By graduation time, Buzzy had become sufficiently hip that parting from Slats was indeed sweet sorrow.

Slats stayed on in Boston working days as a cab driver and nights with a group called the Groovers. The Groovers were a high energy R-and-B band with a female lead singer. Her stage name was Little Cleopatra; her real name was Naomi Witherspoon. Slats was very much in love with Naomi. He loved her as much as he hated the dance steps that the Groovers forced him to do. One night, after a particularly sweaty set, it all came to a head. Slats quit the band and asked Naomi to marry him. She accepted, the band broke up on the spot, and Slats and Naomi decided on Minneapolis as a place to start their new life.

Buzzy, meanwhile, had given the New York jazz scene his best shot but, even though he knew the inside vocabulary, used the arcane handshakes, and practiced under the Brooklyn Bridge, he couldn't seem to crack it. Penniless and spiritually broken, he limped back to his parents' home in Bryn Mawr, Pennsylvania. In a few short months he was without a goatee, saying "I am going" instead of "I be going," and earning a good living as a vice-president in his father's lawn-ornament company. He had seven people under him. One of them was Chicklet. Chicklet's real name was Susan Webster, and Buzzy couldn't take his eyes off her. One thing led to another, and by December she was pregnant with Jason. They had a huge wedding with a society orchestra, and the idea of sitting in never even dawned on Buzzy.

All of this happened twenty years before Chicklet's Princess phone rang and she answered it, hoping it was the rug cleaners. "Is this Mrs. Albright?" said the pleasant voice on the other end.

"Yes, is this Sani-Carpet?" she responded.

"I'm afraid not. This is Rayfield Williams. I'm an old friend of your husband's and I wanted to say hello. Is he there?"

He sounded nice enough, so Chicklet cupped the phone in her hand and called to her husband, who was watching a tennis match in the den. "Honey, do you know a Rayfield Williams?"

"Tell him it's Slats," said the voice on the phone.

"Slats?" she echoed.

"Slats?" said Buzzy. "Are you kidding? Give me the phone!"

Instead of the traditional "hello" or "hi," Buzzy immediately started scatting Thelonius Monk's "Straight No Chaser" into the receiver.

There was a pregnant pause, and then Rayfield spoke in a voice full of control. "They still call you Buzzy?"

"No, man," said Buzzy. "Walter, the dudes I'm hanging with call me Walter. Can you dig that? I mean, what kind of a handle is Walter? Where are you, man?"

"Well, we're in town for just tonight and it's wide open. I thought that maybe—"

Buzzy interrupted him. "You got to come by the crib, man."

"That sounds lovely," said Rayfield. "I'd like to meet your wife and I know you'll enjoy meeting Naomi."

Arrangements were made and directions were given, and Buzzy slumped wistfully into his Barcalounger. Chicklet broke the reverie of his nostalgia. "Six o'clock is four hours from now! How in the hell am I supposed to come up with a decent meal in four hours?"

"We'll just get a couple of pizzas," said Buzzy.

"We will not!" exclaimed Chicklet.

"Chicklet, it's cool. These are get-down people," said Buzzy.

"Quit talking like an idiot and tell me what they like to eat. I need some help here," Chicklet replied.

"Well, I'm picturing barbecued chicken, black-eyed peas, collard greens and . . ."

"Are these people black?" asked Chicklet.

"That doesn't matter," said Buzzy.

"It does to me. I don't have an inkling how to

cook that stuff. I was thinking of a big salad and omelets. But noooooo, you want an Alabama hoedown, so I tell you what I am going to do. I am going to call the catering service and see if there is someone there who knows a pig's foot from a crepe."

"Fine with me," said Buzzy. "Just make sure that it's not a black cook. It won't look very good."

"I'll ask for a Cuban," said Chicklet as she stormed out of the room.

Rayfield Williams was in town on business. Moving to Minnesota was the best thing that ever happened to him and Naomi. He locked his horn in the attic and began work for IBM as a shipping clerk. In five short years he became a senior vice-president in charge of marketing. He never saw his horn again except for the day they cleaned out the attic as they were preparing to move into their new five-bedroom home in the suburbs of Minneapolis. He put the horn in the pile of things for the Goodwill.

Rayfield had five meetings that day, and every one was running late. As six o'clock rapidly approached he decided to give his wife a ring at the Four Seasons Hotel.

He suggested to her that it might be more time-efficient for her to go on ahead of him. He wouldn't be more than half an hour late. She agreed, finished dressing, and gave their limo driver the address.

Meanwhile, the Albrights were readying their

welcome. Buzzy got out all of his old jazz records and put them around the den in a way that looked like they were constantly in use. He lugged their "lawn jockey" from the front lawn to the basement. He took their unread Book-of-the-Month Club copy of *The Color Purple*, put in a bookmark toward the end, and displayed it prominently on the coffee table. Chicklet went through her cupboards and threw out their Uncle Ben's rice and Aunt Jemima syrup. She tore the cover off the *Newsweek* that showed rioting in South Africa. She opened their *TV Guide* and put red Pentel circles around *Webster*, *The Cosby Show*, and *That's My Mama*. She was debating whether or not to circle *Dance Fever* when the doorbell rang.

She ran to the door, saw an attractive middle-aged black woman in a white dress, and jumped to the wrong conclusion.

"Shit," she said. "I asked them to send a Cuban."

Naomi was taken aback to say the least. "I beg your pardon?"

"Well, at least you speak English," Chicklet said, and ushered the speechless Naomi into the kitchen, where she gave her an apron that said DON'T KISS THE COOK. "Cook whatever it is that you people cook, and try to stay out of sight. They'll be here any minute." The doorbell rang again and Chicklet collided with Buzzy on his way to answer it. "They sent a black cook," she told her husband.

"Better than *no* cook," he responded, and they both opened the front door.

It was Rayfield, immaculately attired in a beige turtleneck, blue blazer, and gray flannel slacks. Standing next to him was a delivery boy from The Booze Barn, holding a case of Schlitz Malt Liquor. "Slats!" said Buzzy, grabbing the case of beer and handing it to his wife. He then bounded onto the porch and put an enormous bear hug on his longlost friend. Rayfield responded with the kind of hug one might give to an older aunt. The delivery boy, upon seeing this display of what seemed to be one-sided inter-racial homosexuality, decided not to wait for a tip. He turned and, halfway down the walk, hollered back, "Hey, Albright, somebody stole your lawn jockey!"

"You ought to report that," said Rayfield as they entered the house.

"Right on," answered Buzzy, raising his fist defiantly.

Rayfield held up a bag containing four bottles of vintage Dom Perignon. "Meanwhile, where should I put this?" he said.

"On ice, man," said Buzzy as he read the labels on the bottles. "This shit is some serious shit!"

Chicklet frantically wagged her head, indicating "No, not in the kitchen," but Buzzy never saw it. He was too caught up in trying to be hip around his former mentor. "Mi casa, su casa, Slats," he said as they crossed through the dining room.

When they entered the kitchen, there was

Naomi in her DON'T KISS THE COOK apron staring blankly into the open refrigerator. Rayfield went to her immediately and kissed her on the mouth. "What's the matter, honey? Can't wait for dinner?" he laughed.

Chicklet felt Buzzy's armor-piercing glare and let out a barely audible "Oh my God."

Soon, thanks to the soothing effect of an entire bottle of Dom Perignon and Naomi's inordinate graciousness, the misunderstanding was ancient history. Now the topic turned to something much more immediate. Namely, what to do about dinner.

The idea of going out was squelched by Naomi. "These fellas haven't seen each other in twenty years," she said. "Let them just sit and reminisce. You and I can pool our talents in the kitchen. I'm sure we'll find something."

Both men threw up their hands, indicating "Anything you decide is fine by me."

Chicklet turned to Naomi. "I can't believe how nice you're being about all this!" she said. "I'm going to say this and I hope you don't take it the wrong way, but you remind me of a Negro Dinah Shore." Naomi simply smiled, and the two women repaired to the kitchen. Buzzy and Rayfield went into the den. Buzzy put on John Coltrane's *A Love Supreme*, opened another bottle of Dom, and tried to recapture his youth. After several abortive attempts at hand slapping, Buzzy slowly lapsed back into two things: (a) his real self; and (b) the bottle of Dom Perignon. Buzzy sat there getting snockered while Rayfield talked about the importance of income averaging, profit sharing, and short-term debentures.

Meanwhile, Naomi and Chicklet were almost done with the omelets and tossed salad. "I use the prepackaged croutons," said Chicklet. "It's always a lot faster and a lot less mess than trying to slice a piece of toast."

"So do I," said Naomi.

The girls sat and sipped their champagne while the omelets finished cooking. They became more and more comfortable with each other. Enough so that Chicklet felt she could say just about anything.

"You know the guy that said he had a dream?" said Chicklet.

"Yes, of course, that was Doctor King," Naomi said, smiling.

"Right. Well, he said something about going to the mountain or something like that, and the other night I had a dream myself that had a mountain in it. We were on a ski trip with a bunch of people that I didn't know, and when we got off the chair lift the mountain turned into a pile of soapsuds and nobody could breathe."

"Do you write your dreams down, Chicklet?" asked Naomi in a therapeutic tone.

"Why?" said Chicklet.

"Well, it might be useful if you ever want to find professional help."

Chicklet took a sip of her champagne. "The

only professional help I need is a cook," she laughed.

Their tête-à-tête was broken by Buzzy's stumbling into the kitchen. "Someone's in the kitchen with Dinah," he crooned, slurring most of the words.

Buzzy disregarded Chicklet's warnings and cracked open another bottle of Dom Perignon. The decision was made to eat right there and then in the kitchen.

Rayfield, Naomi, and Chicklet talked freely about public school versus private school, the environment, and the importance of supporting PBS. Buzzy never touched his food and interrupted several times with the same expression: "Mi casa, su casa, honest to God."

Chicklet, Naomi, and Rayfield took their coffee into the living room. Buzzy followed shortly with his glass and the last bottle of Dom Perignon.

It was about nine-thirty when they first noticed the flashlights poking around the front yard. Rayfield went to the window and reported that it was a police car and two patrolmen who seemed to be looking for something. "I'll go check on it," he said gallantly.

"The hell you will, Slats," slurred Buzzy. "You a guess in my house! I'll handle it." Buzzy staggered to his feet and walked into the entryway closet, shutting the door behind him. "I think he's ready for some coffee," said Rayfield as he left to investigate the disturbance.

Rayfield only got about halfway down the walk before he heard the two officers shout, "Freeze!" In a matter of seconds he was handcuffed and sitting in the backseat of the patrol car.

"Pretty far from your part of town aren't you, Jimbo?" said the first officer.

"What the hell did you expect to do with a lawn jockey in the ghetto?" laughed the second.

Buzzy freed himself from the closet and joined the two ladies, who stood at the window in stunned disbelief as the patrol car whizzed away.

"They can't do this to my bro!" shouted Buzzy as he stumbled into the kitchen to get his car keys.

Chicklet beat him to the keys. "We're all going," said Chicklet with authority. "And I'm driving." Buzzy slipped his half-finished bottle into his jacket pocket and soon the three of them were in the Camaro on their way to the station.

By the time Buzzy and the wives arrived, Rayfield had already made his one phone call and the place was crawling with IBM executives and lawyers. The police were profuse and sincere in their apologies. Rayfield was free to go. The last thing he needed was Buzzy bursting into the room and screaming. Buzzy burst into the room, screaming.

"You fuckers!" he shouted. "This guy is the greatest tenor-sax player on earth! Fuck Sonny Rollins. Fuck Coltrane. This guy here is . . . this guy is . . . my man here is . . ."

Buzzy lost his thought at the same time he realized that the bottle in his hand was pouring on his foot.

"Mr. Williams is free to go," said the desk clerk to Naomi and Chicklet. "We're terribly sorry for the inconvenience."

Buzzy got a second wind. "I'll bet you asshole gumshoes listen to shit like Lawrence Welk!" Then he began chanting loudly. "Free Slats! Free Slats! Free Slats!"

"I think Clarence Darrow here might need a place to spend the night," said the desk clerk.

Once Buzzy's paperwork was completed and he was securely in his cell, Rayfield called his limo driver, and he and the two ladies made it home safe and sound.

About a half hour later the police picked up a Cuban man in a chef's suit, loitering outside the Albrights' home. They threw him in the same tank as Buzzy. The Cuban spent the next two hours screaming *"innocenti"* at the top of his lungs, but Buzzy never heard him. He was fast asleep dreaming about the Brooklyn Bridge.

It must have been about four o'clock in the morning when Rayfield realized that he couldn't get any sleep knowing that his old buddy was in the slammer. He went to the station house, bailed him out, and drove him home.

The ride was unpunctuated by conversation.

When they reached the Albright home, Buzzy extended his hand in the normal position. Rayfield shook it politely.

"I don't know how I can ever repay you, Slats," said Buzzy, a bit tearful.

"Send me a lawn jockey," said Rayfield as he closed the power window and sped off to the Four Seasons.

12

Everyone called him Blur. It wasn't short for anything; it was a reference to his extra-thick glasses. Things like that tend to stick out. Along comes a nickname, and that tends to stick, too.

Blur was one of those young white whiz kids that pop up every so often. He won a spelling bee at the age of three, graduated from high school at twelve, and finished his doctorate in biophysics when he was fifteen. It was two years later that Blur shocked everyone by quitting his promising job with the Rand Corporation and heading off to Fort Wayne, Indiana, to study taxidermy.

Blur's only hesitance in leaving home was leaving his parents. Blur's father was a mouse and roach expert with a local exterminating company and never quite understood "where Blur got all them brains." His mother was a cashier at the International House of Pancakes and a prizewinning fudge chef. They gave Blur their blessing and, in return, Blur gave them his stereo and Perry Como records.

It was in Fort Wayne, Indiana, at the Fort

Wayne College of Taxidermy (referred to by the locals as "Stuff-it State") that Blur met Nancy Bennet.

Nancy was the same age as Blur, shared the same passion for taxidermy, and wore wire-rimmed spectacles that looked like they had been cut from the bottom of a glass-bottom boat.

It was a lifeless little parakeet that brought them together. When he was alive and flying around the house, the little budgie had been known by his adoring owners as "Skippy."

Now he was known as "P-322, Make it look perky, on a branch, by Thursday." Dr. Wendell, the head of the bird department, assigned this task to Blur and Nancy.

Because the combination of Blur and Nancy was so exceptional, P-322 was ready by early Wednesday. Dr. Wendell was so pleased with their work that he excused them from afternoon classes. Blur asked Nancy if she'd like to have some clams at Howard Johnson's. Good seafood being a rarity in Indiana, she jumped at the chance.

Blur asked Nancy about her family over clams and coffee. She told him that her mother was an Austrian volleyball champ who had snapped her spine during an exhibition match with the North Koreans and now lived in a full-service rest home in Keene, New Hampshire. Her father, although remarried to a manicurist, also lived in Keene, pursuing a career as a snow-tire salesman. She added that he still made daily trips to the rest home to visit his ex-wife, never forgetting to bring along her favorite cheese. It was a tradition that his current wife had learned to live with, forgive, and understand.

Blur spent the night at Nancy's apartment. It was a first for both of them.

Six months later they were married in a small chapel at the full-service rest home with all five parents present, each one vowing to stay close and "keep this a family."

The happy couple found a modest apartment over an insurance office and set up house. Nancy did her best to make the dimly lit flat into a real home. She ordered "His 'n' Hers" bath towels, put a No-Pest strip in both rooms, and painfully thumbtacked shelf paper to every shelf in the place.

She also went to the pound and got a little black-and-white kitten. She named the kitten "Baby."

Blur took on the task of provider with equal nobility. He secured a night-shift job at a local bakery as a doughnut icer. It wasn't the exciting life of stuffing varmints he had dreamed of, but it paid the bills for now.

Blur's shift was six to ten PM, getting him home at night about ten twenty-five. Nancy would serve him Ritz crackers and Campbell's tomato soup and ask how it went at the doughnut plant. Later, they would watch Carson, taking turns playing with Baby.

Baby became an increasingly important part of their lives.

By year's end the little apartment was

crammed with Polaroids of Baby and hundreds of cat toys.

Life was going along pretty darned well until the night that Blur lost most of his nose. Apparently his failing vision had deteriorated to the point where even his Coke-bottle lenses couldn't compensate. Attempting to grab a fresh bowl of icing, he leaned over the conveyor belt and was struck in the face by the doughnut holer.

In all, about forty dozen doughnuts were ruined by the profuse bleeding, so Blur's boss had no recourse but to fire him on the way to Fort Wayne Eye, Ear, and Nose Hospital.

Blur was stitched up expertly by an elderly Costa Rican nurse who had gained her deftness with a needle and thread during sixteen years in a baseball manufacturing plant.

Once the bandages were all in place, Blur could have easily passed for the Elephant Man's brother. He found a pay phone in the emergency waiting room and called his wife with the news.

"All of it?" she exclaimed.

"Not quite," he explained in a voice understandably nasal. "I still have most of the right nostril. Can you come and get me? They made me leave the car at the doughnut plant."

There was a long pause.

"I can't right now," she explained. "Baby is acting real funny, like she's lonely or something, and right now I'm all that she's got. You understand, don't you?"

Blur assured her that he understood and took the bus home. It was well past two when Blur finally stumbled up the stairs to his apartment. His wife had long since gone to bed with Baby and was still in her REM cycle when she heard the keys in the door. She had been dreaming that she was in an igloo, surrounded by black-and-white cats and hundreds of boxes of doughnuts, so when Blur entered the room she was still pretty much in "La-la-land." Blur turned on the light and Nancy rolled over to see what, to her, looked like an enormous bandaged thumb with eyes in it. She let out a scream that rivaled an air-raid siren.

They say that in times of crisis everything seems to go in slow motion. Once Nancy screamed, however, the following events occurred in what felt like a millisecond.

1. Nancy bounded from the bed right into Blur. (Neither one was wearing glasses.)
2. Blur put his hands and knees up to protect what was left of his nose from her attack.
3. The angle of collision was such that Nancy was virtually catapulted into the kitchen, where she landed flat on her back on top of a pile of cat toys.
4. The night watchman in the insurance office below them was aroused by Nancy's scream and scampered up the stairs with his loaded .22 caliber pistol in tow.
5. Blur started rummaging through the chest of drawers for his other glasses, realizing that he was useless without them.

6. Baby dashed for the front door of the apartment.
7. The night watchman arrived at the door. He took one look at what seemed to be a robbery in progress. He instinctively fell to one knee and drew his revolver.
8. The sound of Baby screaming under his knee caused him to panic. He fired his gun.
9. Blur found his glasses and then dropped them. He bent to retrieve them and felt a sickening throb in his left buttock as the bullet passed through.
10. Nancy tried to sit up and realized that she couldn't.

Nancy's spine had snapped at the same exact point as her mother's. After six weeks of medication and rehabilitation she found herself, with Blur's help, in the same room as her mother in the full-service rest home in Keene, New Hampshire.

Blur's injury was minimal. It was a very clean wound; the bullet had passed straight through and lodged in one of Baby's rubber mice. At Blur's request, Dr. Wendell was summoned from the Fort Wayne College of Taxidermy. Using their combined expertise, Dr. Wendell was able to remove a bit of fatty tissue and skin from Blur's butt during the closing-up operation and fashion a splendid new nose for him. The nose was never what you would call functional; Blur couldn't smell a cat fart in a closet, but it looked great.

Then something miraculous happened.

We've all heard stories about sightless people gaining an incredible sense of hearing—the senses compensating for each other. That's exactly what happened to Blur. His inability to smell caused his eyesight to repair with amazing alacrity. By year's end he was better than twenty-twenty. Soon he could spot acne on an ant. At Dr. Wendell's insistence Blur applied his new-found vision and long-standing intelligence to the field of microneural surgery. Blur, once again the whiz kid, was an expert in six months. His skill was such that neither Nancy nor her mother could ever find their incision scars.

It was a snowy December day in Keene, New Hampshire, when Blur saw his wife and mother-in-law walk out the front door of the full-service rest home. No chairs, no crutches, no nothing. Everyone in both families was tear-choked, but the real gushing came when Blur presented Nancy with Baby mounted in one of her favorite positions.

13

The Crisco Kid

Candy Matheson had the second biggest breasts in the ninth grade. The first biggest belonged to Shirley O'Leary, but she'd already been scooped up by one of the senior boys.

Monty Milsap waited a full year for his voice to change completely before he even spoke to Candy, but he was in love with her the whole time.

One Thursday evening after really only picking at his chicken pot pie, he excused himself from the table and went to his room. He flopped on the bed and stared at his Phillies poster. Tomorrow? Should he talk to her tomorrow? Was he ready? He went to his desk, took a piece of notebook paper, and drew a vertical line down the middle. On the left he wrote the word "Pros," and on the right he wrote the word "Cons." The list looked like this when he was finished:

Pros	Cons
1. I'm taller than she is.	1. Everyone is taller than she is.

Pros	Cons
2. I don't sound like Jim Nabors anymore.	2. She hates me and doesn't even know it yet.
3. I have my learner's permit.	3. She'll go out with me and everything will be great and then her father will get transferred and they'll move away and the whole thing will be a waste of time.
4. I've got great hair.	

It was his confidence in his hair that turned the tide for Monty. Monty worked very hard on his hair. He knew every curl, twist, part, and wisp. Truth be known, it was fairly wimpy blond nondescript hair, but with the help of half a tube of Brylcreem, he was a walking work of art when he left the bathroom in the morning.

Monty went to sleep that night a man resolved. He made a "flat person"—that was his mother's term for laying out the clothes you wanted to wear the next day—and set the alarm a half hour early so he would have more time with his hair before his father had to shave.

Monty killed the Brylcreem that morning and went off to find his life mate.

Since Candy was in the ninth grade and Monty was in the tenth, their paths didn't cross that often during the day. Monty had memorized her paths, however, and knew just where and when to make his move. Candy always left the lunchroom early so she could go to her locker before biology. The halls were usually empty. Perfect, he thought.

Candy was in a semicrouch by her open locker when Monty sauntered up with a half-eaten ice-cream sandwich in his hand.

"Hi, Candy," he said as nonchalantly as possible.

"How come you know my name," she said blankly.

Monty wanted to scream out, Because I've done nothing but dream about you for the last year and can't believe I'm really talking to you and want to marry you right now. He didn't, fortunately. He simply said, "I read it on your charm bracelet."

"Oh, yeah?" she said, reaching into her locker for her biology book and a mason jar containing a fetal pig.

"We did our pigs last year. I'm a sophomore. My name is Monty," he said, nibbling the inside of his lower lip.

"You have any more gum?" she asked.

Monty ignored her remark and came straight to the point. "Listen, you wouldn't want to go to the basketball game tonight, would you? We're playing Oberlin."

"I know we are." She smiled proudly. "My boyfriend is a starter for Oberlin. He's a senior."

Monty heard the sound of enormous steel doors closing in front of him and felt his heart tumble straight down and lodge in his rectum.

"So, okay, fine," Candy continued.

"Okay. Fine what?" said Monty, totally baffled.

"Okay, you can take me to the game. Kevin has to go on the team bus so he can't take me anyway. This'll work out perfect. You take me there and pay for me and I'll go home with him. You don't mind sitting on the Oberlin side, do you? They're gonna win anyway, 'cause Kevin is soooo good."

She crouched in front of her locker and took out some more books. She turned to the dumbstruck Monty and smiled sweetly. "Well?" she said.

Monty stood over her at her locker, peering straight down the neck of her sweater at the little crease that separated the two sides of heaven. Somehow her offer, though hardly the "evening of magic" that he had dreamed of for so many months, was gaining strength.

Monty knew that if he backed out he'd regret it for the rest of his life.

"Well, I guess that sort of kind of maybe sort of sounds like fun," he stammered.

Candy picked up her books and pig jar and gave Monty a tiny kiss on the cheek. "Super," she said, and ran down the hallway. Monty felt his legs turn into feathers.

"Because it's against the law, that's why," said Monty's father over chicken pot pies. "You need a licensed driver over the age of twenty-one in your car with you. Either your mother or myself."

"You can still do the driving," his mother chimed in. "In fact, Arnold," she said to her husband, "why don't we both go and it'll feel like a double date to little Kimmy?"

"Her name is Candy, Mom, and she's not little." Monty left the table to wrestle with this problem and soon found himself face-to-face with a much larger one. He was out of Brylcreem.

It was ten of six, and all of the various emporia that might carry Brylcreem in Ridgeville were closed. Monty started to panic. He locked himself in the bathroom and started going through the medicine chest in hope of finding some sort of substitute.

All Dad had was Vitalis, and that was out of the question. It made his hair look like limp lettuce and, worse yet, it smelled like his dad. His mother had some Aqua Net, four cans of it in fact, but you had to have your hair in place before you could use it. She also had some stuff called Waveset. Monty knew that in a terrible pinch he could use the Waveset. The only problem was that once it dried it made your hair look and feel like pie crust.

Pie crust, he said to himself. Why didn't I think of that? He bounded from the bathroom to the kitchen and grabbed the family-sized can of Crisco.

He locked himself in the bathroom again,

put a big glob of Crisco in his hair and started combing.

Unbelievable, he thought as his comb started its sculpting. This stuff is *better* than Brylcreem! Monty finished his hair in record time and even added a few new wrinkles that Candy would have to be blind not to notice. He was so "hair secure" that he didn't even mind that both of his parents were going with him to pick up Candy.

Monty's parents did their best to be inconspicuous after Candy was picked up, but it was impossible with Monty driving. His father was on him every inch of the way. "Both hands on the wheel, Monty." "Start your turn signals." "Downshift, for Christ's sake!"

His mother had a few suggestions of her own, mostly in the area of "Slow down." She reacted to every red light and stop sign by slamming her foot into the back of the seat where Candy was seated. Monty had hoped that Candy might scootch over next to him, but his mother's kicking was so violent that Candy was forced to wear her seat belt.

The game had already begun by the time they reached the high school parking lot. "Don't forget the emergency brake," said his father.

"And give the keys to your dad so you won't lose them," added his mother.

The Ridgeville side of the gym was almost full, the Oberlin side almost empty. Monty knew that he would stand out like a horse in church if he sat on the Oberlin side, but he had promised. Worse yet, the only way to get there was to walk across the court during a time-out. A time-out was called, and Monty and Candy began the long walk to the Oberlin bleachers. Monty thought about shielding his face but he knew his hair would give him away. Already he thought he could hear the cat calls. "Hey Monty! Wrong side!" "What about Kevin, Candy?" "Monty's got a girlfriend!" And the simple but provocative, "Milsap, you asshole!"

Finally, after what felt to Monty like a forced march down the Burma Road, the young couple reached their seats. Monty had hoped for the top right corner of the bleachers where the light wasn't so bright, but Candy prevailed. They sat at center court with Kevin's young brother. "We're gonna kill Ridgeville," said the younger brother to Monty, "and afterward my brother's gonna kill *you*." Monty thought about *Star Trek* and how they were able to just "beam" themselves somewhere else. That's when the buzzing started. It wasn't the buzzing of human voices. It wasn't the buzzing of the heating system. It wasn't the buzzing of the buzzer. It was the buzzing of flies. Lots of them.

Monty had overlooked the fact that Crisco, despite its wonderful cosmetic qualities, was basically a food. Humans never eat Crisco. They just put it in things to eat. Flies, on the other hand, like it straight, and Monty represented a banquet spread out on a hairy tablecloth.

At first it was just annoying. Annoying enough, however, for Candy to move so that Kevin's brother was between them. Then they started coming like locusts. In a matter of seconds Kevin's brother and Candy both moved to the far end of the stands, as did everybody else who had been seated around them. Monty was seated all alone in the middle of the Oberlin bleachers, his head covered with flies.

It wasn't eat and run for the flies either. Once they landed on his head, they found themselves mired in the thick layer of Crisco and unable to extract themselves. It was like a miniature version of the dinosaurs and the tar pits.

The good news is that by 1:06 left to go in the half there were no more living flies in the Ridgeville gym. The bad news is that Monty had become a brunette.

The last minute crawled by like a funeral motorcade. Before the halftime buzzer had even finished buzzing he was in the boys' room staring into the mirror.

For some reason all he could think of was that his head looked like those oranges stuffed with cloves that his mother made as Christmas gifts.

He tried combing out the carnage to no avail. His hair had become so grizzled that the comb teeth snapped like twigs in a power mower. Meanwhile the boys' room was filling up with full-bladdered teenagers. "Is that supposed to be funny?" said one of them. "Hey look, it's the Human Flypaper," said another.

Monty dashed from the rest room, formulating his plan on the run. He would go to the locker room and take a shower. He even had Brylcreem in his gym locker. He'd be good as new by the second half. Monty heard the steel doors close again as he approached the locker room. It was locked and there was a Magic-Markered sign that said *"Team Meeting—No Visitors."* Through the door Monty could hear Coach Ratski screaming at his players. Ridgeville was down 46 to 68 at the half, so he had every right to scream.

Monty stood slack-shouldered and considered various ways of killing himself. He decided to lie under the back tires of the Oberlin team bus and was on his way to do just that when he heard the hissing of the visitor's shower room. He tried the door.

It was open. Did he dare? Could he make up a story that they would buy? "Hi, guys, I'm Monty Milsap and I'm on the road with Bruce Springsteen. He's sleeping in the car so I thought I'd take a shower." Not bad, but not good either. "My dad is one of the referees, and he said it would be all right." Perfect, he said to himself as he ducked into the visitor's locker room. He stripped quickly, grabbed a towel that said Oberlin on it, and brazenly strutted into the showers. It seemed for a moment that Monty's luck had changed for the better. The shower room was so filled with steam that all you could make out were shapes under the pounding water. He found an empty spigot, lathered up, rinsed, relathered, rerinsed and was ready to go when the shower next to him shut off and the room was suddenly clear of steam.

"You shouldn't take a shower at halftime," said Monty to the misty figure in front of him. "It'll sap your strength."

"I want to look good," said the figure. Monty turned his shower off, and as the steam fell to the floor he could see he was staring right into the eyes of Kevin Forsythe.

"Hey, aren't you the wimp that was sitting with Candy?" he snarled.

Monty was all set to lie and tell the Springsteen story but, for some reason, he went for the truth.

"I just brought her because she lives nearby and you had to go on the team bus anyway and she loves you a lot and she's going to go home with you."

"Oh, really?" Kevin started to laugh.

"Honest to God," said Monty.

"Well, that sure is news to me and to Kathy."

"Kathy? Who's Kathy?"

"My girl. Dickhead."

"Well, then what's Candy?" asked Monty.

"She's a frigid fourteen-year-old who wears falsies!"

Monty snapped like a comb tooth. "She is not. She's the girl I've just been through hell for!" he screamed, and shot his left foot into Kevin's midsection with more force than his mother had ever kicked a car seat.

Kevin took the thrust with the ease of Marvin Hagler. Then he wound up for the counterattack. Monty quickly turned on the shower as a diversionary tactic and ducked away. Kevin tried to change his angle in midswing, lost his balance on the wet floor, and fell with a thud. Kevin's radius was a clean break; the ulna was just a hairline fracture.

———

Monty didn't even comb his hair. He just dressed as fast as he could and ran back to the gym to sit with Candy.

"Kevin's been hurt," he said with just a hint of a smirk.

"No he hasn't," Candy responded.

"Oh yes he has," said Monty with a full smirk.

"Your hair looks different," said Candy.

"My hair doesn't matter," said Monty. "It's just hair."

Without the services of Kevin Forsythe, the Oberlin Eagles found Ridgeville a much tougher opponent and ultimately lost the game by two points.

Monty never told Candy about Kathy. He didn't have to.

She saw Kathy sitting on the bench with Kevin, kissing him, rubbing him, and owning him.

Monty and his parents drove Candy home. She cried the entire way, and Monty used her tears as an opportunity to hold her hand. It was the hand holding that he would never forget.

Later that night, as he slumped into bed, Monty stared at his Phillies poster. He accepted the fact that he never got his hands on either side of heaven but held it open as a possibility. A real possibility. As for reality, he shut his eyes and took comfort that he was responsible for an 88 to 86 upset for Ridgeville.

14

White Dawn

If there was any kind of shooting war, we never knew about it. Later on we figured it must have been fought on two giant computers, like one of those international chess matches in Iceland, and their computer won. Fair enough. Maybe our computer will win the next time.

Anyway, we were all sitting around the breakfast table watching the *Today* show when word came that the Russians would be running things around here for a while. As you know, this had long been forecasted, like earthquakes in California, but when it finally happened the world didn't exactly stand still or anything. They didn't have to switch presidents or send Congress home or even change the regularly scheduled TV programs. Outside of a few malcontents from Alabama, everybody seemed to take it in stride. "Something different for a change," is the way that my wife Agnes summed it up.

Of course, our two teenage boys, John and Jack, got a little hot under the collar. They were both Guardsmen at the time—still are, in fact—

and didn't like the idea of taking orders from a non-Minnesotan, let alone a non-American. Agnes tried to pound some sense in their thick heads. "What are you going to do, grab the .22 from the hall closet and fight 'em off at the city limits?" she asked. That's actually what they had in mind, but after they saw on TV what the Reds did to those boys in Alabama, they decided to take a wait-and-see attitude. "Use a gun, go to Gorky" was the jingle we kept hearing. It was catchy and the boys soon had it memorized.

We were hardly through with the morning coffee when there was a knock on the front door and we got our first taste of doing things Russian style. They are not big on "how-are-ya's," that's for sure. Agnes thought the way they just barged in and started rummaging through our knick-knacks was downright rude and didn't hesitate to tell them, though the boys and I tried to keep her on ground level. They apparently got the message. The more Agnes screamed and beat on their chests, the more they laughed, and soon we were all laughing, including Agnes. Nothing like a good laugh to break the ice with strangers.

It was about that point that I realized I had just the thing to make these boys feel right at home. Vodka. I pulled a bottle out of the liquor cabinet and they took to it like all outdoors. They'd never had it with orange juice, and we'd never had it with beet juice, so it turned into a real cultural-exchange program. We all sat around watching *The $25,000 Pyramid* and getting sloshed to the gills. I finally called in sick at the office. There was no way I was going to sell any sprinkler systems today!

Finally, the head guy, Ivan, which he swore was his real name, handed me a piece of paper that apparently was our marching orders. I couldn't read Russian, but I had served in the Big One and knew a reassignment sheet when I saw one. I got out the Rand McNally map of the U.S. and started pointing out locations. There was a lot of confusion, what with Agnes and the boys trying to squeeze in their two cents, but we finally figured it out. Our Russian friends wanted to go to California and surf. We were on our way to a special desert rendezvous near Truth or Consequences, New Mexico.

From what little I could make out, the trip had all the makings of a Boy Scout jamboree for the whole family. Camping out under the stars. Boiling your own water. Using nature's commode. I liked to camp and so did the boys, so we were excited. Agnes thought that Minnesota or Wisconsin had more to offer for the avid outdoorsman, but the Russkies were dead set on New Mexico. They probably knew something we didn't.

We hardly had time to gather up our hiking boots before the bus arrived. First stop: Hubert Humphrey in downtown Minneapolis. Apparently lots of people were on their way to these Boy Scout jamborees and a football stadium was the best in overnight accommodations they could come up with on such short notice. I don't know why the Holiday Inn people couldn't help out; they probably had their hands full with out-of-town guests from Moscow. Anyway, they had cots set up for everybody and free soup that was mostly turnips. Frankly, it wasn't the best soup I'd ever had, but who could complain? It was free. We settled in and found plenty of new friends to play cards with and swap jokes about the soup. A week or two had passed before you knew it, and I realized I didn't miss work a bit. I did miss my favorite TV shows, but we made up our own version of *Dynasty* and had a good laugh. As Agnes said, "Something different for a change."

New Mexico turned out to be a big disappointment. First, the train trip was horrible. We have really let train travel slip in this country, if the cattle car we were stuffed into is any indication. And the people that ran the camp in New Mexico were not as friendly as those Russian boys that came to the house. They must have been from another part of Russia, a part where not only education was important, but also "reeducation." They were sure big on that. For twelve hours a day we took reeducation classes in everything from tractor repair to the Withering Away of the State. John and Jack really took to this new way of looking at things, and before long they were wearing brand-new National Guard uniforms with CCCP on the back and living in a condo in town. We were so proud of them!

After six months or so both Agnes and I and most of the people we knew were getting fed up with turnip soup and the heat and the "Volga Boat Song," and from what we could tell, the State didn't seem any more withered than before. We knew we had to get the Russians to start seeing things our way or this could get old fast. We all gathered out by the latrine ditch one night and drew straws. I got the short one and was elected to "reeducate" our visitors from the Ukraine. I thought I was biting off more than I could chew, but I accepted the challenge. I couldn't see any harm in it.

Step One: I got friendly with the commander, Marshall Ogrovdinikova. I laughed at his jokes and helped jerryrig a surefire sprinkler system for his private beet garden, and he was beholden to me. He didn't seem like such a bad fellow after you got past his irritating habit of slapping you in the face every time you mentioned Sylvester Stallone. He was a little stiff and humorless, sure, but so was Agnes's brother, a state building inspector in St. Paul. That didn't mean I was going to blow his head off with an M16, though I thought about it once or twice. You have to get along to get ahead. It works every time.

It doesn't take much to "reeducate" someone to relax and have a good time here in America once you put your mind to it. Even a stick-to-the-manual sourpuss like Marshall Ogrovdinikova soon warmed up to an occasional after-dinner round of croquet or kick-the-can, and it wasn't long before he was a self-declared sports nut and a devoted *Lifestyles of the Rich and Famous* watcher like the rest of us. You just don't realize just how much America has to offer in the way of entertainment and recreation until you walk a few miles in the shoes of a Russian. One day your only leisure-time option is to drink enough potato juice to kill a cow and squat-dance until you fall over. The next day you have a wall-sized TV, a VCR, a plentiful supply of snack food, and a par-three golf course in your backyard. Marshall Ogrovdinikova did not have trouble deciding which life was for him.

If you got a lemon, make lemonade. That's what Agnes always says, and the marshall finally took her advice. With the help of a couple of contractors out of Albuquerque, he turned our bleak desert outpost into something to be proud of. A retirement village. Everybody pitched in to build the bike path and the square-dance area, and the marshall thought the way we all got along in organizing the softball league was more communistic than the Politburo itself! When the time came, we had no interest in going back to Minnesota, even if my old job was waiting. We had made a new life here and so had our Russian hosts. Soon we couldn't tell each other apart.

As for the big picture, I really don't know who's in charge at the moment. I saw some Saudi Arabians running around Washington the other night on TV. Maybe their computer won and they're steering the ship for a while. What with all the sprinkler problems you run into in the desert, I don't have much time to keep up.

All I know is that, in the long run, the American way of life will prevail. Why? For one main reason. It's just a whale of a lot more fun than the others.